ALMOST
OUT
OF
GRACE

David Yanez

Copyright © 2009 by David Yanez

ISBN-10: 0-9772194-3-7
ISBN-13: 978-0-9772194-3-8

Library of Congress Control Number: 2008939340

Printed in the United States of America.

RevMedia Publishing
PO BOX 5172
Kingwood, TX 77325

www.revmediapublishing.com

A ministry division of Revelation Ministries in Houston, TX

www.revministries.com

Book cover design by Febe Menendez
Author photo by Timothy Dip
Front cover photo by Jessica Leza
Copyediting by Jeanette Morris, First Impressions Writing
Services, www.firstimpressionswriting.com

I DEDICATE THIS BOOK TO

My son's David, Nathaniel and Matthew whom I love and see greatness in each of you. God has great plans for you! My daughter Faith who is a precious jewel that God has given me to cherish. My wife who is everything I need, want and desire in a woman. Thank you for giving me the time and encouragement to get this book done.

CONTENTS

Section 3   The Commitment of Partners

Preface

Have your ever felt that you let God down in the way you handled your dating or marriage relationship? How about that déjà vu feeling? That you've had the same (bad) experience before, but you can't help repeating what you know doesn't work. Emotions about our relationships are constantly shifting from highs to lows. If we know we are not in the right relationship, we still try to convince ourselves or our partner otherwise. Sometimes that convincing leads us away from God, Christian friends, family, and the church. Does this describe you? And if it does, do you ever wonder if all your rationalizations and poor choices have exceeded the limits of God's patience with you—so that you are almost out of grace?

If so, I've written this book for you.

Introduction

When I consider the amazing statistics of divorce in America today, I am shocked to see how many *good people* are torn apart through divorce or separation. I think a bad divorce (I never heard of a good divorce) can devastate a family as nothing else can.

Yet, divorce happens all the time. Whether you are sitting in your cubicle at work or sitting in a pew at church, you will know or hear of someone who is getting divorced. Sometimes the news comes as a surprise to you; other times you have seen it coming. Amazingly, in the place and lifestyle we choose as Christians, where marriage is supposed to be sacred, we are falling apart. Sometimes it seems as if couples in the church are splitting up quicker than we pastors can marry them. Truth be told, being a Christian does not exempt anyone from the problems all couples have.

This book will focus on relationships—single and married. I hope I can help to reveal who you are in your relationship—what you are contributing, either to its success or its failure. No counselor, pastor, friend, or family member can give you every answer to your situation in one or even a few sessions. Just like one book will not do the complete job either. But it is my hope that these pages will give you godly insight into what you can change. Because honestly, we all need change to save our relationships and marriages.

"Think about this for a moment" is a phrase I use on my "Midwatch with the Rev" radio and TV show. I ask the audience to think about something just before the break. This is not only to get listeners to stay tuned in for the next segment, but also to get them to look at something within themselves. I also say, "Be honest with yourself," because being true to ourselves is the first crucial step toward healing. Most of the time, all anyone needs to effect positive change is an honest answer to an honest question.

Shortly after the first airing of our radio and pod casts programs, we hit a ratings gold mine. We had decided to focus for a month on relationship topics. From broadcasting in near obscurity, we went to being among the top ten downloads in big markets like New York. Our pod casts Web sites nearly tripled in downloads overnight. I don't think it really hit me until our toll-free prayer line went ballistic one Sunday afternoon about 2:00 p.m. I had prayer request after prayer request from people in troubled relationships. I spent hours on Sundays praying for people.

Our show was only thirty minutes long, but we received calls for three hours afterward. The response made me wonder about the rest of America. How many people out there are hurting from failed relationships? My eyes were opened even wider after getting several e-mails—from California to the Netherlands. Our shows didn't broadcast in those areas. So the listeners must have picked up the live stream or the pod cast. People wanted to hear what we had to say about relationships.

Besides jobs and health, relationship is the most thought about, talked about, scrutinized about, cried over, researched about, pouted about, and chased about topic in the world. Think about this for a moment: Money can be made again. Houses can be replaced. Jobs can be replaced. With your health, you can do only so much; the rest is by God's grace and good genes. That leaves your relationships—and there is only one of you to love, one of you to share and one of you to live a meaningful life with someone designed just for you.

People expect too much flash and lights when it comes to relationships. So much beauty and seduction is shoved in our faces through television and movies. We too easily forget that we are supposed to be valuable to someone in a relationship. We are supposed to mean something to someone. If you get nothing else from this book, remember that you are important—a treasured gift from God!

Recent news programming featured people committing suicide—in offices and residences, even at parties. Some even went so far as to take hostages and execute them before killing themselves. If you read these reports in the newspapers or on the

4

Web, you will learn that many times these distressed people were having relationship problems. Be it going through a divorce or separation, not being able to communicate with the opposite sex, or depression and insecurity, when they came to the point of hurting someone, they had obviously reached their emotional rock bottom. The tears have dried up. The heart is drained and tired.

Psychologically they are tapped out. There is no self-esteem left in the tank. All that is left is paranoia, which takes over any rational thinking that might still exist.

I want you to know that whenever a person resorts to hurting another person (even just a little) emotionally, physically, or spiritually, it is because he or she is desperate—desperate about losing. These outbursts or rages could also be signs of something deeper within the heart. Desperate people need many hours of love, counseling, and godly deliverance.

As you read this book, look honestly at yourself. I really pray something in here grabs you. My heart goes out to the person who is still waiting for his or her true love. I know God holds everything in His hands for you and those you love.

SECTION 1

EMOTIONAL BEHAVIORS

CHAPTER 1
Desire

I have been married to my beautiful wife for over twelve years. I thank God for giving her to me. She is everything I wanted and more. She is the woman God handpicked for me. I am grateful for the beautiful family we have together. I also thank God for pulling me off the draining emotional roller coaster of desire for a spouse.

Thousands of Christian singles go through it every day—pondering the question, "Is this the one Lord?" The desire to find a spouse becomes so strong that it takes over your life. I know, because I was one of those Christians. Desire works like a magnet— dragging and pulling on you until you get into a relationship with someone. In spite of the love you feel for the people around you, without a "relationship" you feel like something is missing. What? What is behind the desire pulling at you?

While on this path to find the person who God has handpicked for you, you will make big mistakes. You will allow yourself to be pulled prematurely into wrong relationships. Because the drive is so strong, many times you will be the one doing the pulling. Sometimes even the dragging. Maybe you will meet a person whom you believe fits in your life perfectly. Friends and family agree with you. Then because you think it's God's will, you pursue this relationship at all costs—even at the cost of your spiritual discernment. When you start making spiritual sacrifices to keep that relationship together, you need to stop and examine if it is really from God.

Desire—does it have its place?
Is desire for a spouse from God? Does this desire ever leave? If not, will it ever become easier to deal with? I can guarantee that you have heard this scripture before: "Delight thyself also in the Lord; and he shall give thee the desires of thine heart" (Psalm 37:4). Pastors have preached and taught on this verse for decades alongside the topic of finding a spouse. Many of us cannot help

feeling that the verse doesn't do us justice. We follow God with all our hearts and we still have no one.

You may be an anointed man or women of God. You may be a successful businessperson, or you simply may be going about life the best you can. Yet, you are still searching for that special someone. Desire will make you wonder if you have done something wrong. You will dissect everything in your life, over and over again, trying to analyze why you are still alone. Desire will also make you think twice about every relationship you enter. You may meet someone extra special— possibly at work, church or even at the gym. Because of desire, your mind might have become clouded. Instead of letting God's timing open up this special relationship, you will jump through hoops to get the relationship going *now*. In fact, you start moving a little too quickly. You have already decorated the wedding cake in your mind, picked a place and time to make this union official, and started a guest list. Okay, maybe not that far, but you get the point.

Desire will make your normal relationships abnormal.
Let me explain. I know if you ask any guy the question, "Which four words do you hate hearing from someone you are interested in," you will get the same answer. Men hate hearing these four words from a woman: "You're a great friend." Why do guys hate that word *friend*? Because it is a marker of the position of the romantic possibility (or, better said, impossibility) of the relationship. You may have some good friends of the opposite sex. He or she may even be your best friend. But the moment you want something more, that friendship becomes abnormal. Especially if the other person wants friendship, but not romance.

Desire makes us see what isn't real.
Desire can make us place the wrong person in the high position of the recipient of our deepest love and devotion. Because we have a lack of understanding of that position and an overwhelming emotional pull to have a spouse in our lives, we unwittingly assign and ordain the next "whomever" to be our God-destined bride- or groom-to-be.

Please understand, I don't use the words "God destined" lightly. I respect the sacredness of marriage. In fact, I am one who believes God has made a unique and beautiful person just for you. I truly believe this person exists for every one of you singles reading this book right now. That man or woman is also searching for you. Call me an old romantic, but I believe a heart pounds and cries for you just as yours is pounding and crying right now. I have prepared scriptures to show you what the Word says: that God understands the insanity you feel—the overwhelming desire to have a special love in your life. How does God understand this? How does He know what you are going through?

Desire is God-given
He is the one who gives that desire. Desire for a spouse came from God. In the Scriptures it says: "Whoso findeth a wife findeth a good thing, and obtaineth favour of the Lord" (Proverbs 18:22). In this verse, God acknowledges that finding a wife is something not to take for granted.

This task is difficult emotionally, socially and physically. You will become drained and feel exhausted. But it is a good thing you search for, and it's is a good thing when you find it. God honors the courage, desire, and obedience you have shown to get on the path of marriage. He so much honors it that He bestows His favor on those who persist in the search until they find. Can you imagine having the favor of the God of all creation? It's true! He is concerned about your life, and if He is giving you His favor, it means He is well pleased that you found a special person. It means that He does have someone especially for you. God giving you His favor is a great thing.

Only God can guide you to that special person and reveal him or her to you. I will share a few stories I have heard over the years about this type of revelation. When I taught on this subject, I called the sermon "The Great Treasure Hunt." I felt finding a spouse was like having a map that required us to put together clues and pieces to find a hidden jewel. Your wife or husband will be that treasure in your life.

Revelation on this subject came to me when I was traveling back to my ship in Long Beach, California. I was about twenty years old at the time. I had been in the navy for a few years. My heart had always belonged to God, but I began to feel a need for someone to be a part of my life. Truth is, many guys in the military marry young and out of emotion, loneliness and need. Some of these marriages make it; others don't. I sat next to a businessman on the plane to Los Angeles. We started to make conversation about what we both did as the plane taxied across the runway. We learned we both were Christians and had a call to ministry. He paused for a second during our conversation. He then looked at me and said he could see the desire all over me. I thought he meant the desire for ministry, but then he told me the desire he saw was for a wife. I was surprised I looked that desperate!

He went on to remind me about Adam and Eve. Adam did not have to run around or impress anyone. He didn't have to scream and whine. He didn't have to search or ask if this person was the one. He didn't have to act depressed or troubled because life was passing him by. All he had to do was obey God and rest in the Lord's provision. Adam got his wife when he rested. God brought Eve to him while he slept. I still think this story is awesome. Having God bring a person to you is a lot better than your holding one up to Him for His approval.

Back to the beginning
If you look at the story in Genesis 2, you will learn three important truths.

First, God knows your need. He knew Adam needed someone before Adam even knew. "And the Lord God said, 'It is not good that the man should be alone; I will make him an help meet for him'" (Genesis 2:18). Adam didn't finish naming everything until verse 20. Why is this significant? Because before Adam could name everything, he had to see everything in the Garden of Eden. He had to cover every square inch. That means up every tree and under every rock. He had to scour the hedges and fields to make sure everything got a name. At the end of the day, we read in Genesis 2:20 "….but for Adam there was not found an help meet for him." Adam had just seen everything that walked, flew, crawled, and jumped. Yet nothing in creation fit him. In that time of working and seeing everything around him, Adam developed a desire or a need to have someone with whom to share his life. This need was something new to him. Ever since his creation, he had been in close relationship with God, who always provided everything he needed, without his having to ask for anything. He had food, water, shelter and a beautiful, perfect life. Sound familiar? Some of us have everything, much like Adam had, except the spouse of our dreams. But the difference is, Adam wasn't searching for her. He was keeping himself busy in obedience to God by naming all the creatures. So before Adam could even ask God for a wife, God prepared him to have his need met. In this obedience of being about his Father's business, God gave him rest.

Second, God has a plan for how He will provide and bring this person into your life. He has a specific time and place for this to occur. He has preordained this and will make the provision. The truth is, if you have a desire to have someone in your life, then the plan to bring that someone into your life has already been made. How do I know this? Let's look again at the story of Adam and Eve. After sitting in the garden, even though it was so beautiful and had plenty for him, he still needed something. By our culture's standards, Adam was rich. He had plenty of anything he wanted. Technically, he was a caretaker, but in reality, a king of his own destiny. Yet with all the abundance, he found one lack. Deep down inside, he knew he really wanted to have someone with whom to share all of it. He wanted someone special. He didn't find it in the fields. He couldn't see it in the air. He had to depend on the Lord. God already had the plan. Adam felt the need, but God made the provision. That simple!

Genesis 2:21-22: "And the Lord God caused a deep sleep to fall upon Adam, and he slept: and he took one of his ribs, and closed up the flesh instead thereof; and the rib which the Lord God

13

had taken from man, made he a woman, and brought her unto the man."

Think about it. Adam woke up and standing beside him was a beautiful woman who was waiting for him. He didn't have to go find her. God brought her! God walked her into his life! God knew exactly where Adam lived. He didn't lose his address. Oh, if only it was that simple for all of us. The Word of God doesn't tell us how long Adam had to wait until God put him to sleep. Neither does it say how long he slept. But it does show us the provision and plan God has for all of us who have a godly desire.

The third truth to remember is that when God brings you the special person, your spirit, heart and mind will know it. You will have no doubt about it. No one will be able to tell you differently. Look at Adam's confession in Genesis 2:23. "And Adam said, This is now bone of my bones, and flesh of my flesh: she shall be called Woman, because she was taken out of Man." Immediately, he knew she belonged to him. Everything in him said that this one was for him. God did not have to tell him about the entire process of the rib removal. He presented her to him and Adam felt the connection. Remember, Adam was not a caveman. God created him with a high intellect, able to calculate and reason. He needed no help to identify what his entire being felt—this woman was from God and was part of him. His heart felt it, his mind knew it, his spirit confirmed it and his bones yearned for it.

Is he, is she, the one?
How do we know when we find the right person for marriage? To try to answer that, we need to ask a few questions of ourselves. Does the person make you feel better about yourself? Does he or she build your faith? Can he or she complement your vision? Does this person truly love you? I know these questions sound a bit tough. But if you've found the right person, these questions should be easy to answer. Truthfully, when we have God's perfect love in us, it's easy to love almost anyone. It's also easy to love the wrong someone. In fact, there are so many hurting people out there today that many of them would be happy to "rent" that special space in your heart—for a while. But as most renters do, they move on

when the commitment rent gets too high. You don't want to worry every day that the person you're with might be gone the next morning.

But I can't let go!
If you find yourself unable to let go of the wrong person, you need to find out why the passion in your heart seems unbearable and life without this person seems impossible to deal with. You need ask yourself if you're holding onto the *idea* of having him or her, or if God has brought the provision. Ask yourself—have you fallen in sin? Desire can make us do crazy things. You will see your commitment level to God drop if sin has entered the picture. Church becomes less important. You make excuses to go see him or her when your responsibilities are supposed to be elsewhere. You make yourself available to this person night and day.
You will be so attracted to or pulled toward this person that you will ultimately put yourself in situations that will cause you to sin.

So why can we feel so deeply for someone that living without them seems impossible? Because any time you place someone in the special place in your heart, you unlock all the devotion, love, commitment, joy, and fellowship reserved for your spouse. Remember that God has made you able to love someone without any limits, just as He loves us without any limits. When you pour out that love on someone undeserving because of premature desires, you will become dissatisfied. You risk never knowing the completeness God intended marriage and love to give you.

CHAPTER 2
Real Romance

Many of us have a great desire for a spouse, and maybe that person is part of your life today. Nevertheless, he or she would be just another beautiful person if a few of the essentials to a great relationship didn't exist. One of these essentials is what I call Real Romance. Without it, a relationship isn't able to stand strong in times of testing. What is your idea of romance?

Physical Attraction

Some of us might say romance happens when you are unable not to be around someone. He or she must be with you or you just hurt. Romance is a day full of flowers, candy, jewelry, and sweaty palms. The attraction between one another is almost animalistic. If there aren't chairs flying and bodies crashing into tables, then it's not genuine. If you're not passionately lip locking at the beginning and ending of each day, then something's wrong with the whole relationship. I call this the KFC relationship, "its finger lickin' good"—all about the physical.

This kind of romance is based on sight, touch, and sound. Thousands of people have been trained and trapped into thinking this is how a relationship must be or it's not really love. Many of us tend to confuse romance with physical passion.

Understand that physical "signs and wonders" do have a place. However, a relationship based solely on this will not survive. The minute passion stops so does the trust. This is when the questions begin to rise up about the validity of your love for one another. Let's be honest. Loving on someone physically is easy. It's exciting. It's adventurous. But if you hold to the value of a strictly physical relationship, you're setting yourself up for a great heartbreak.

Let's say the love you have for one another is strong—strong enough to survive when the passion and physical attraction slows down. The danger is that most marital affairs are based on the same precepts of physical attraction—adventure and thrills. The devil has to paint something alluring enough to cause you to experiment. That's why it's called temptation, because it looks too good to pass up. The answer to many of the questions men and women ask when a relationship succumbs to temptation from outside lies within the physical basis of their relationship. Why do we fall out of love? How can he/she just get up and leave? What can't you be with me anymore?

If a person wants only a physical relationship, it's a sure bet they will go from relationship to relationship. Just remember, if you decide to steer down this route of physical relationship, one of you will find someone more exciting and thrilling down the road. Maybe both of you will. God has a better plan than that for you. Why do you want to spend hours of the day wondering if your problems will ever resolve?

It's all in your mind
Another kind of romance is mental. No matter how much a person tells you he loves you, you still need more proof to believe it's true. I see people in this type of relationship all the time. Sherry sits at a table having lunch with her girlfriends and quizzes them incessantly about Bryce. Do we look good together? Does he look handsome enough? He called me only twice yesterday, what do you think that means? He hasn't brought flowers in a week.

People in these relationships need to see a mental picture to gauge if it's going to be successful and are constantly in an overly emotional state of mind. This kind of romance quickly drains the excitement out of a relationship.

The main problem with this kind of romance is that it second-guesses. You might have a truly good person in your life—maybe one whom God sent. But because you refuse to accept what doesn't fit into your mental picture of "the perfect one," you nit-pick the relationship into an early grave. You have conditioned your mind not to accept the truth. This often causes depression as finding Mr. or Miss Right in time seems impossible.

18

In time? Yes. This type of romance often sets a timer. Sometimes there's an exact date or age these people want all this to happen for them. Many times it doesn't. We can't set God's time clock for our lives. All we can do is serve and obey, believing the promise is around the corner.

The major flaw in this relationship scenario is that mental romantics want too much out of something too soon. For instance, if a girl doesn't receive a phone call or flowers often enough, she immediately begin to suspect something is wrong. Mental romantics allow past failures to haunt them. Although they want a good relationship, they are usually the one to break it off because their own minds prevent it from succeeding.

Mental romantics often generate a lot of false hope for those around them. They have preconceived ideas about how long to stay in relationship with someone. Devastation is harsh and swift when they leave a close person without notice. A mental romantic needs much encouragement, exhortation, and reassurance to keep them in a relationship. The person giving this comfort is usually the spouse or spouse to be, who genuinely cares for that person. But to no avail, the comforter is told that someone else would be a better match. Mental romantics can be the most successful and beautiful people you will ever get to know. It seems that nothing should stop them from having a sincere and dedicated person in their lives. Yet, they are still alone. My heart goes out to this type of person. They need a lot of prayer and comfort to make it through the day without succumbing to depression.

I feel good
The last type of romance is the feel-good romance. This type is typical of a guy or gal who believes he or she is in a Spirit-led relationship. To be very honest, it's tough to make the call on these relationships, because often the person's spirit may truly be sensing something from the Lord.

Feel-good romantics usually know from the get-go if a relationship is not right for them. They may even know why they feel the way they do. Maybe they recognize a certain personality type that clashes with theirs, or maybe they know themselves well enough to recognize impending disaster. They may have had something happen in a previous relationship that raises a red flag. But for some reason, feel-good romantics choose to ignore their better judgment. They go forward and begin a relationship, which they should avoid, because they want to feel good.

Maturity in God counts for something. As you get older, you tend to get wiser. Nevertheless, no matter how mature a person is, he can fall. He can make a bad decision. He can hurt others.

The feel-good romantic has several criteria he looks for in a relationship. The first one is the need to *feel* he is in love. I used to watch a TV show with my older sister when I was a kid called, "Love American Style." The one thing I remember about the show is when the guy and gal were about to kiss each other, fireworks would explode in the air on the screen if it was true love. Some of us believe this myth—that unless you see fireworks popping in the sky—it isn't love.

Feel-good romantics will tell you they don't feel peace. Many times this is true, especially if sin is in the relationship. You will never have peace, even when that person may be the one for you, if sin continues to control your relationship. Peace is the feeling in your heart that the relationship is right. When someone doesn't feel at peace, he or she will be restless until the relationship ends. But in reality, if the relationship is meant to be and feeling peace about it is possible, consider the possibility that confusion is keeping peace at bay.

The feel-good romance keeps everyone from feeling good. That's sad, because in most instances, these relationships actually come close to working out. In fact, because you're attempting to open yourself up spiritually, you may be close to getting the answers you need. God wants you to have great feelings in all of your relationships. Whether it will make it all the way to wedding bells is up in the air—at least until His timing is right. Sometimes the best way to keep a relationship intact is to avoid putting too many expectations into it prematurely.

More often than not, the physical, mental, and feel-good romances will have insecurities, jealousy, and fear imbedded in them. That isn't real romance.

Then what is Real?
Real Romance means your special person is totally in love with you. He or she totally trusts you, and knows you would never intentionally cause harm. Real Romance means you want the best for your spouse. You want to make him or her a better person and stronger in his or her relationship with God.

Real Romance doesn't keep a stopwatch on where you're going from day to day. It doesn't have your routes timed or give you a twenty-five-question quiz when you get home. Real Romance doesn't pick up the phone to screen your calls. Doesn't listen in on the extension to see what you're talking about. It doesn't check your e-mails or voice mails to satisfy its curiosity that you're being faithful. It doesn't wait outside your gym to make sure you are actually working out. Doesn't visit you on girl's night or guy's night out to make sure you're with the girls or the guys. (This behavior describes the Christian stalker, which we will cover in chapter 4.)

What is Real Romance? A little of what I shared above, but more of what I am about to quote. John 15:13 reads: "Greater love hath no man than this, that a man lay down his life for his friends." This is the definition of love that comes from heaven. Since marriage and the relationship between God and the church are parallel, I believe that unless the person you're involved with has the total love of God for you, the marriage may not work out. He needs to be the one who is crying tears for you as much as you do for him. She needs to be totally accepting and forgiving of all your past mistakes. Your spouse can't afford to be haunted by your past relationships, just as much as you can't (more on this in chapter 20). Give me the one who prays for me; give me the one who will stick with me through the good and the bad times. Give me the one who is faithful to God. Because a person who is faithful to God will be faithful to me and treat me like a child of God, not a possession.

The greatest love of all

Think about it for a moment. Greater love has no man—greater love has no woman—than this: that he or she loves you unconditionally and will go the distance for you, no matter what. This scripture, of course, is a preview of Christ dying on the cross for us. He gave His life so we may be saved through His atoning death and resurrection. In addition, if marriage is an example of the relationship of God with His Church, then we need to have a man or woman who would say, "I will die for you." That may seem extreme. But is it really? Shouldn't we all expect to marry someone who will unselfishly agree live and die for us?

Of course, we don't want our spouse to die. Nevertheless, if you could find a spouse who purposes to follow God, take care of you, and build your relationship, wouldn't that be awesome? To know that level of dedication and love is beyond compare. My God, my wife, and my family are what I live for. Success, money, and status all come in last place, because when I follow God and take care of my family, He promises to add the rest.

Remember, my friends, Real Romance will not take advantage of you. It will not make you feel less of a person or a Christian. It will not degrade you. Real Romance will build you up and give you a stronger outlook on life and God. No matter what you think, you never should have to please somebody to make them love you. Real Romance has boundaries and respect for one other. It doesn't control and manipulate. Real Romance betters both parties equally, even though each person is in his or her own process of growing.

One flesh
I shared earlier that a physical relationship has its place in Real Romance. Now let me attempt to explain. In Real Romance, it is important to have a good physical relationship. Your spouse or spouse-to-be should make your heart excited. He or she should be attractive to you. Your romance should be adventurous and thrilling. But the foundation of your relationship should not be set on that alone. The place it should have is one of intimacy and exclusivity. You should want intimacy only with your spouse. You should have sexual desire only for your God-given life partner.

Real Romance should bring out the complete love you are capable of giving physically. It should give you joy to share that part of you with your spouse. Romance should be a part of your daily walk. You should be to express your love without fear of rejection. The emotional outpouring of just a simple hug or gentle kiss may be the greatest strength in your entire marriage. Just how you look at her or hold her—just how you hug him and tell him you appreciate him—may be all your spouse needs. When all is said and done, from deep inside the heart should come an outpouring of love, which will in turn become physical because that's the natural response. Your entire being inside should want to be complete physically with your spouse, forsaking all others.

CHAPTER 3
Trophy

After searching highways, valleys, mountains and the mall for a perfect spouse, you think you might have found your prize. You have searched for several months, or even years, for this person. You have prayed all night for a tangible revelation. You cried buckets of tears for the chance to have someone in your life. Finally the time has come. You can now raise your hands in victory, because you have the won the prize. You have the trophy you worked so hard to get!

Take it easy...
Are you sure? Or are you just tired of searching? Did you settle? Or is this person actually the one God prepared for you? How many relationships has it taken for you to declare that you have a winner? Whom did you hurt in the process? What happened to those former relationships? Are those girls, those guys, still following God?

We need to be careful in our relationships with other believers. Especially since some may get offended or embarrassed and leave the church, or worse, leave the Lord, because they are hurt by a failed or broken relationship they thought was from Him. Finding balance between accountability to God and letting Him lead vs. allowing your exuberant emotions take over is difficult. A hurt heart is problematical to heal; you can't just reverse pain. So when you finally get this trophy, ask yourself some serious questions. What sold you on the person? What made you feel you could hold up him or her like a prize? Did you find someone just so everyone could approve? Besides what everyone is saying, what makes this person stand out to you spiritually?

Even though you are excited to have this person in your life, you need to be honest with yourself. Does this person care about you and your relationship as much as you care? If God has brought someone to you, there will be certain aspects of and benefits to the relationship.

25

What benefits?
God knows your needs. The right person will complement your life. This doesn't mean someone who speaks pleasantries. This word means: to complete. If you need a man in your life to be a strong prayerful man because you lack the prayer language and endurance, then God will supply. If you need a woman who can live in a jungle in India or off Rodeo Drive in Beverly Hills, then God will supply. This complementing goes beyond the major, life-changing decisions. The small things are just as important.

You might be the type who needs encouragement on a daily basis. You may need affection because you're not the type to give out affection. I will tell you this from experience, opposites attract because they work better together for God's purposes. It's true. God will put an outgoing person with a more introverted one because He knows they will balance each other. He will put a talker with a shy one. He may also put a zealous risk taker with a careful planner. Why? God has a plan. Just look at your family and friends. You will notice changes that have occurred after they have been together for a while. Each one's character and personality rubs off a little on the other one.

My wife and I are perfect examples of opposites. I am the risk taker and the outgoing personality. She is the shy and cautious one. Because she has rubbed off on me, I am a better equipped to walk this walk. Likewise, she has seen by my life to be encouraged to take a risk now and then.

To know if you have found your trophy to hoist up and say "thank you Lord," let's review a short list of attributes that might be indicators that you have found Mr. or Miss Right.

- This person should take away the fear that you may have of being alone in life. Only God can give you the peace to fill that void. Therefore, if you have found Mr. or Miss Right, that void should be filled.

- This person schedules time to be with you. You don't have to remind him or her that you need to get together. Remember, you are not a burden! You're not a bother. You shouldn't have to set an appointment. Your planner shouldn't be the only one with scribbles and scratch outs. Both of you should work together to arrange time to be with one another.

- You shouldn't have to impress this person to get him or her to stay with you. Keeping the interest and love flowing shouldn't be hard labor. Your future spouse needs to genuinely want you for you. He or she needs to be happy being with you. It shouldn't be a "settle for" relationship. A marriage will go only as far as each person will take it. Marriage will not succeed unless the two people in it are trying to succeed.

Men's and women's hearts are revealed when someone close to them begins to declare his or her love. When you say, "you are everything I ever wanted," they will either rejoice or run. No kidding. This statement will set off the safeguard alarms they have set up. It will overwhelm them with joy or give them panic attacks. You're not just the giver and he or she is not just the taker. Both of you should make equal efforts and equal sacrifices. If someone has put in your mind that sacrifice is a dirty word, you are destined to fail, my friend. Every relationship will be only as successful as the degree of willingness to sacrifice.

As a side note, if you're spoiled or overly pampered, you will have problems in your marriage, because every day will not always go your way. This goes for guys and gals. I have known couples where both had been the spoiled child in their birth families. Sacrificing is difficult for "spoiled brats" because neither will yield. Each one wants to do his or her "own thing." For some, that arrangement may work. One will go hang out with the guys— the other with the gals. They start enjoying different hobbies, which is fine as well.

But this arrangement prevents the establishment of balance early in their marriage—no set standards ensuring each will yield to the other. They continue to be happy with running around doing everything and anything they want to do.

Then all of a sudden, a baby arrives. A baby is God's great curve ball. This baby will expose the weakness in any marriage. Why? Because it takes discipline and a servant's heart to raise a child. Your true hearts will be revealed when you become parents. All of sudden your life will change. Hanging out with the guys and doing what you want is gone. Some have trouble understanding that. They have trouble grasping that life will no longer be the same. Now don't get me wrong; it's good to have friends and hang out with them. In marriage, however, you need to be available to your spouse. If you don't discipline yourself early, you will rely on lame excuses and wreck your marriage. What's the best advice I could give to pampered couples? Yield! Yield! Yield! Yield to God. Yield to your spouse. Yield to your heart.

I believe when you find the perfect person, one whom God has prepared for you, you have received a gift from God. If God the Most High is giving you a gift, it will be a blessing in your life; it will make you a better person. You will not make steps backward or always have to apologize. This person will complete you in areas you didn't know were void. You will want to give of yourself unselfishly. You will want the best for him or her as well. You will hurt when he or she hurts. You will know God gave this special one to you because you will love him or her as God loves you. He or she will become your morning and your evening— someone you enjoy being with and around. Your gift will give to you the same compassion and commitment, and more, in return. You'll know you've found the right one when you feel the love coming back to you!

CHAPTER 4
Christian Stalkers

I believe there are different ways in which God shows us whom we are to marry. Some of you may be overwhelmed with excitement when you receive the news. Some will feel dread. If God gives you this knowledge, you have been entrusted with an awesome responsibility. Imagine knowing from the Most High God whom He picked for you. What will you do with that information?

Unfortunately, many men and women of God allow emotions to overtake them instead of the Spirit. Many Christians become stalkers of their future promised husbands or wives. I want to share with you a couple of stories about some men and women of God who received specific revelations from the Lord about the identity of their future spouse. The two outcomes were very different.

Don and Georgia
"Don" was in the navy and attended a local church near the base. He, like most young people, had a core group of friends who fellowshipped regularly. In this group, he became best friends with a young woman named "Georgia." They palled around together—visiting people and praying with them. Don enjoyed his friendship with Georgia, but he had a romantic interest in someone else—another young lady in the singles group. He was awestruck. Stars in his eyes! You know, the goo-goo eyes that make you float around the room. I like to call it the Rudolf syndrome. You might remember the animated story of Rudolph the Red-nosed Reindeer. In a particular scene, a female reindeer tells him he's cute. Rudolph responds by flying farther than any reindeer while screaming, "I'm cute!" at the top of his lungs.

Don shared his feelings about this other girl with Georgia. She was happy for him because she knew he was happy. As a good best friend, she tried to influence this girl toward the young sailor. But nothing worked. She didn't have goo-goo eyes for Don at all.

29

He was so hurt in his heart. He cried out to God each night, "Why doesn't she want me? Why doesn't she have feelings for me?"

One night Don prayed a different prayer: "God, I will accept your will. This pain hurts too much. This void is painful to my friends. Those who carried it know and those who are still carrying it feel it." Then one day while he was at home, still sad and eating Cheerios, the women who owned the house he lived in as a border noticed his downcast mood. She told him he needed to go out and do something. Later, his friends from the church group called and invited him to a youth rally. He didn't want to go. But sometimes God uses friends and family, even strangers, to help us during mental and spiritual depression. And when we are in our deepest depressions or frustrations, often the best course of action is to get out of our caves and get some fresh air. God will talk or move on our behalf, but if we stay bottled up, we will not see the answers we are seeking.

Don's landlady, a strong Christian, insisted he go to the meeting because she believed God had something for him there. His friends picked him up, even though he looked like he really didn't want to go. At the service, during the middle of praise and worship, one of the ministers called Don up to share the Word. As he stood on the platform delivering an exhortation, God began to shine on him. His friends who were watching began praising God. Then something amazing happened. The Holy Ghost started to speak!

But the Spirit didn't speak to him. He spoke to Georgia, who was sitting in the crowd. The Holy Ghost whispered her name. She stood still and whispered back, "Yes." The Holy Ghost said, "Do you know who I am?" She said, "The Lord." He went on to say, "Before I tell you what I have for you, I declare that your sister will confirm this for you at home, so you'll know it's from me." Then Holy Ghost shared, "Pick up your head and behold. Your husband-to-be is on the stage right now." Slowly she picked up her head to look up at the stage. There stood Don, who was starting to speak.

She immediately screamed, got up, ran to her car and drove home. When she got home, she walked in crying. Her sister was there and asked what was wrong.

Georgia wouldn't answer her. Then her sister told her, "The Holy Ghost told me your best friend was going to be your husband." Georgia screamed again.

An hour passed when Don came knocking at the door. Georgia's sister said that Georgia really didn't feel like talking right then. He went home with a peace and release on the whole relationship situation that previously had him feeling so depressed. When he got home, he felt led to pray for Georgia. Later, he called her to see how she was feeling. He still had no idea what the Holy Spirit had revealed to her. While they were on the phone he said, "The Lord just told me that what He shared with you is between you and Him, and you are not to tell me until He shows you it's okay."

As the days went on, she shared with her sister that she thought of Don as good friend, but not as a boyfriend. She wasn't attracted to him all. Nevertheless, God began to open her eyes and heart toward Don. Eventually she shared with him what the Lord had shown her. Don responded calmly, assuring her that if that was God's will, then He would make it happen. In the meantime, he would be content to date her and remain her best friend. Today they are happily married and pastoring a church together.

Notice that neither Don nor Georgia forced the relationship. From the beginning, God orchestrated and forged their two lives together for His divine purpose. This example showed how two mature Christians handled a relationship. They were yielded to the Spirit and followed His guidance.

Even though we may assume someone is to be in our life forever, God may have different plans. God is able to give us insight. The danger comes when we think we have the insight and we are sick in love with someone. We refuse to let go of the thought that this person belongs in our life. We wrestle with our belief that we have heard the voice of God.

We begin to get confused and even become a bit desperate. Why would we become desperate?

One reason is that we want someone so badly. Another is that we become hardheaded and our pride refuses to allow us to yield.

Phil and Judy

"Phil" and "Judy's" story is an example of this hard-headedness. Phil was a minister and just coming out of a failed relationship. He was still dealing with his broken-heartedness when he met Judy though mutual friends. In his previous relationship, he felt he always had to please the girl to ensure she would stay with him. This time, he was hoping for a commitment—not another situation where he felt used. Judy was never happy in any relationships. She believed she had already let the right one get away, and that she had missed the chance for true love. She felt that her failure to remain pure in past relationships combined with her parents being divorced would doom her in marriage.

Phil and Judy were two people who genuinely loved God and followed Him with all their hearts. As they started to date, Phil quickly assumed Judy was "the one." After much praying about it, he felt God was directing him toward marriage. He prematurely told Judy his revelation. She had no such revelation and thought he was crazy. His strong assertion created too much pressure on someone so uncertain about herself. Shortly thereafter, she decided it wasn't working out, and she ended the relationship.

Then began what I call Christian stalking. Phil started to take matters into his own hands. He showed up at her work, her church, and at the gym. He called her daily, asking her to meet with him. Even though she told him it was over, he couldn't take no for an answer. Despite everything he tried, the relationship never came into existence the way he believed God had planned.

32

Over the next year or so, because of Phil's insistence, he and Judy fell in and out of relationship. Eventually, sexual sin took place and problems between them got worse.

Through it all, Phil refused to let go and Judy was firm in her resolve that she couldn't ever commit to marrying him. The result was heartache on both sides—not the happy ending either was wanting.

Read the signs

So what are the signs of the Christian stalker? Not wanting to take no for an answer; refusing to listen to the other person's wishes. Jealousy, scheming, stalking and refusing to accept that it's over— these are the main components of a Christian stalker. Any time you see these characteristics in a relationship, you need to stand back and see if God is actually in the relationship. Hearing God will be almost impossible while in this mode of stubbornness. Even close friends and family will have difficulty getting through to you.

How does loving someone with your all your heart turn you into a stalker? Often it begins following a disappointment—like being paranoid about losing someone. You go from desiring to have someone in your life to becoming obsessed. You become so determined to get someone in your life that you begin to stalk him or her.

Let's be honest and call stalking what it is. You show up at her home or you're always conveniently around the corner. You go over the line and impose your will in her life. Remember, it takes two to make a relationship. No matter whom you want in your life, it ultimately has to be with mutual agreement. You can't force anyone to love you. And when your love becomes obsession, it's time to search your soul. Following or shadowing someone should raise a red flag. Why are you doing it? Why don't you just let go? Just turn the car around! Simple to say, but hard to do? Then you've stopped listening to your own reasoning. That's when you know you have become a certified, card-carrying Christian stalker.

Let go!
Our hasty actions can be the reason God withholds His blessing from our relationships. No matter how much it hurts to hear it, you need to let go. Let it go now before someone is hurt more than mentally. In every bad relationship is a moment when you should just walk away.

Nevertheless, some of us pass up that moment and try to hold onto something that will never grow. Why drag it on? Why hurt yourself even more?

You deserve better than that, my friend. Let God heal your hurt. Get to feeling better about yourself, and then let God bring the right someone into your life. He wants to bless you.

CHAPTER 5
Fairy Tales

When I was younger, I used to preach a sermon called "Fairy Tales" to youth groups. I thought the title was unusual for teens, but it made my point well and they responded positively to it. In fact, the young people who heard this at church asked me to give them tapes of the sermon. To my surprise, they were taking these tapes into their schools and playing them for their friends, who then asked for copies. They even played the tapes during study hall so the teacher and other students could listen.

Amazingly, I didn't get any complaints from the school board or faculty. These kids were hungry for someone to give them insight about relationships. They were engulfed in the emotional fairy tales our society promotes, and they wanted some help! They were tired of being in and out of love. You remember those days. Your heart belonged to Jessica on Monday and by Friday, you were with Angela. I believe in those blissful times of puppy love, we were told fairy tales about finding a partner for life.

Happily ever after?
Who in America doesn't know Cinderella? It's a great story. A young woman being mistreated by her stepmother is rescued by a handsome price and given a life she deserves. Who wouldn't like that story? Who wouldn't want to be in her shoes? You know what they say: "If the slipper fits!" a true prince will come to save you. I think we all can say that at one time or another, we wanted someone to save us from our hopelessness. We may have even conjured up what this prince/princess would look like. We may have even imagined how he would rescue us. It doesn't hurt to dream and be imaginative about our romantic life, especially if you're still waiting for the right person to come into your life.

The problem begins when we put too much expectation on what a person has, or needs to have, to qualify to hold your hand in marriage. If I asked you to describe the perfect man or woman for you, what would you say? Good looks, good job, good heart, and a little bit exotic?

Many guys would jump and scream for a supermodel. Most gals would swoon over tall, dark, handsome, and rich.

Imagine now that God gave you your perfect guy or gal, right down to every detail. He or she is exactly what you wanted. Do you think there would still be problems? Do you think because your husband or wife has the exact job or lifestyle you desire that there won't be hard times too? Problems will occur in any relationship, because "perfect" or not, two people are trying to learn about one another and trying to make their two lives into one. That's the goal. A good marriage takes work.

Many of us can write our own fairy tale story from our past relationship history. We have as much drama as any book or movie. In fact, we have more sequels than *Halloween* or *Friday the Thirteenth* put together. They all seem to waiver between the romance genre and the horror genre. We have been broken, rebuilt, and broken again. Our past loves have been everything from great to pathetic. Some got away; others ran away. Each one of us can tell story after story—enough to fill every movie screen in America 24/7—365 days a year.

God's grace is limitless
Why do we need a hero or a heroine? Because our inner hearts tells us there is someone special waiting. This special person will be your hero. Don't be short sighted as to how God can deliver.

When I was in the navy, God told me something profound one night as I stood watch. He told me to tell His people not to limit Him. Don't limit His love, His reach, His plan, and His ability to help us. Don't limit His grace for you and miss the right relationship He has ordained. God sometimes sends something—or someone—your way that you simply pass by without notice of its significance.

Consider the biblical story in 1 Samuel 16:1-13. We see that when Samuel went to anoint a king out of Jesse's family, he expected a strong great man to be the anointed one. As all the sons of Jesse passed before him, he kept saying, "Neither hath the Lord chosen this [one]." God had told him not to look at the outward appearance, because He looks at the heart. Soon Jesse brought David from the field to pass in front of Samuel. When David passed by the Lord responded, "Arise, anoint him: for this is he."

God had only one in mind, but seven others had to pass by first. Just like in our relationships, my friend, several have passed by, but only one will do. Wouldn't it be great if one day God just said to you, that's the one? Just go be with him, with her. If our minds are clouded with outward expectations and premises, we will miss His voice about the heart of His choice for us.

Change the way you think

I think the biggest problem in this entire relationship search is unrealistic expectations. At no other time in history have we been so desensitized about sex, romance, and love. We see too many videos, movies, magazines, websites, photos, TV commercials, and TV programs that parade a false image of love.

We have sexual content shoved in our face in almost every other commercial. Spam arrives with pornographic material attached to anyone with an e-mail account. Nearly every music video portrays some raunchy, barely-dressed man or women dancing erotically. Viewing adult movies or porn has become as simple as flipping on the Internet. It's no wonder love like our grandparents or parents had has not been instilled in our hearts and minds. We may have had a good upbringing with good moral family values, but when we allow ourselves to mingle with the sexual addictions and wooings of teenage pop icons, it's no wonder our love and romance relationships are in such a mess. We must change our perception of what is acceptable. The world is lying to us.

Face the fact—your thinking needs to change. God has reserved that seduction and lip smacking for your spouse, not for just any person that you bring to your life. Why tempt yourself with false images? Why make yourself vulnerable for weak relationships? Weak relationships will never progress to anything worthwhile unless true expectations are established.

R-E-S-P-E-C-T

Once I visited a church's singles night at the pastor's house. That night they played an old movie about two people who fell in love. I think it was an *An Affair to Remember*. We were asked a question about one of the scenes—the couple's first kiss. It took place on a staircase on the outside of the ship. The actual kiss was off camera. The shot captured just the feet of him approaching her, then one of her legs rising up as she (assumedly) stretched to meet his lips.

We all knew he kissed her, and we didn't think much of it until the pastor asked us a question. "Why didn't they show the kiss?" Several people guessed they couldn't show a kiss on camera when that film was made, which wasn't the reason at all. I answered according to what I felt about the entire story to that point. The director knew the importance of the first kiss, but he also treated the characters, who wanted love so badly and who had been through many ordeals, with great respect. He wanted the scene of the kiss to be a sneak peek for the viewing audience—to represent his view of how special, how sacred, real love was supposed to be. He also paid homage to the privacy that romance and affection was due.

Many of us have lost respect for love and romance. The sacredness has gone. Real love and romance doesn't mean your dating life should be dull and boring. It does mean that to truly love someone, you need to respect him or her.

Respect includes listening to and honoring the wishes of the other. Selective listening doesn't work. You need to take heed of what your girlfriend or boyfriend is telling you. If he needs space, give him space. If she calls it quits, then let her go.

Nobody can force another person to stay in a relationship against his or her will. Respect is saying good-bye and not forcing a dead issue. Respect also demonstrates maturity in a relationship. Yelling and screaming (which we will cover in chapter 10) is a sign help or time apart is needed.

God doesn't want you to make a habit of leaving a relationship for another one. But He does want you to look into your heart. You know your attitudes and temperament. You need to be honest. Are your fairy tales the reason your life partner has not arrived yet?

SECTION 2

HURT IN RELATIONSHIPS

CHAPTER 6
Whom Do We Hurt?

Getting hurt is probably not on the top of the list of attributes we look for in our relationships. Nevertheless, hurting a person we are close to will eventually happen. No matter if you are in madly in love or simply care about someone, you will eventually hurt him or her, even if it's over something simple. That's just part of the nature of relationships.

Although there are many types of hurt in relationships, the one I want to talk about is sexual sin. Sexual sin is one of the chief causes of strife and hurt in dating relationships. No matter whether you are saved or not, sin is sin. I know if you aren't careful, temptation will get the best of you.

When premarital sexual activity begins, relationship problems become intensified. Once sin has occurred, the door is open to hurt. Both people can ask for forgiveness, believe they are forgiven, and build from the failure. Nevertheless, typically one of the two people can't let go of what happened. One of them will have a problem with the relationship after sin has entered. The other may take the sin too lightly.

Actions speak louder than words
Sin sheds light on the true condition of a person's real heart. He can say he loves you ten times a day, but if he doesn't prove it by his actions, the words are empty. Proving it doesn't mean having sexual intercourse. Proving it means not hurting the one you love.

Realizing that hurting someone is inevitable gives you the ability to stop yourself from that behavior. Typically, a person who doesn't want to hurt you cares more for you than a person who willingly and intentionally hurts you. Now I am not saying that someone who truly cares for you won't hurt you, but that if it happens, it's unintentional. Understand that in every one of us is the ability to make the choice to stop hurting someone.

Do you really want to keep from hurting people you say you love? Do you want to keep from damaging them and their walk with God? Yes, God can heal them and rebuild their lives. But do you care enough not to put someone through that agony? You say you do care that much, but do you care enough to refrain from intimately touching someone you aren't married to? Once the sin starts, it's impossible to stop until one person or the other chooses to stop. Is your physical desire so great or important that you can't stop?

Are you looked to as the man of God—the leader in the relationship? Is there a high spiritual expectation for you? You might see all the stop signs, yet you don't heed them. You go forward with sin. Why don't you stop? It's easy. Just walk away. But the passion and the drive are too strong, you say. Your will replaces God's will. Or, you may even have convinced yourself that your sinning is God's will (more on this in chapter 13). When you start going blind with physical passion, it is hard to see the dangerous road you are on.

A domino effect
If I could put all the people you will eventually hurt with the fallout of your sexual relationships in one big line, would seeing their faces help you stop? Think about it. We are not just talking about the person you are involved with right now. We are including everyone who knows you.

King David's struggle with sexual sin
Let's look at 2 Samuel 11:1-7, the story of King David and Bathsheba. While walking on his rooftop one evening, David saw a beautiful woman bathing. She was married, but he sent for her anyway and had sexual intercourse with her. She became pregnant. David called her husband, Uriah, back from the battlefield so he would sleep with his wife and hide the results of David's sin. Uriah refused the comfort of his wife's bed while his fellow soldiers were waging war for Israel. David then tried to get Uriah drunk, sure that he would then desire his wife. But Uriah remained loyal to King David and spent the night with the other servants.

David sent him on his way back to the battlefield with a letter to Joab, the commander. The letter said to send Uriah into the hottest battle so he would be killed. The plan worked, and Uriah died defending his king. After his widow mourned the days required, David took her as his wife, and she bore a son to David.

The story continues in chapter 12. Nathan the prophet confronted David about his sin. David cried out and confessed that he had indeed sinned against God. Nathan told him he was forgiven and would be spared, but the child would die.

Sin always hurts or disappoints someone you care about and respect. Let's consider all the people in David's life who were hurt because of his decision to sin. He was the king. He knew the law. He loved God with all his heart, yet he still decided to go through with the sexual sin.

Look at Nathan the prophet. He loved David, yet I am sure he was shocked about the whole incident. He was sad and hurt that David was so foolish. Nathan knew David had a grave weakness.

You will lose the trust of others when you sin. Because of your actions, you can hurt innocent people and friends. What about Uriah? He was innocent and devoted to the king and God. He trusted David with his life. He didn't deserve to die. Yet because he put all his trust in David, he ended up betrayed and then dead.

You will hurt those who trust you and respect you. How about Bathsheba? Although she wasn't innocent in the affair, she did have to do what the king told her to do. He knew that he had absolute authority over her. Everyone reverenced the king. Because of her obedience to the lustful king, she ended up in a tragic love triangle.

Sin affects our families! What about the baby? I think this pain runs deep. That would be hard to deal with as a parent— seeing your child become seriously ill because of your selfishness.

I am not saying God will strike down your children or family members.

In these times, we destroy our own families in divorce court. Can you picture your child's eyes staring at you, expecting you to explain your actions? What will you say?

Self-inflicted pain
Beyond hurting those in our circle of influence, I think we hurt ourselves the most. It takes forever to get over our mistakes. After sinning, it's typical to feel you can never get back to your former spiritual high. Sin tarnishes the trust and commitment level between you and God. Sin causes separation from God. Repentance must take place. You must seek God, repent, and pray for restoration of your relationship with Him.

Even though God is merciful and forgives us, our hearts, minds and attitudes don't forgive so easily. God forgives us the moment we ask for forgiveness with a true heart. We will never forget when we were saved, but we will always dread the times since when we have fallen. You will habitually wonder what life would have been like for you spiritually if you hadn't sinned. You will always feel like you lost a step or two that can't be regained. People will inadvertently remind you that you're not as you were years ago in your excitement for Christ. Trust me when I say this is a trick from the enemy. The devil wants you to think that something weird has happened to you and that you're flawed. He will keep reminding you of your failure and your weakness. Why?

One reason is to make you doubt the same God who forgave you. Another is so you will think the forgiveness Jesus gave to us through his blood is not for your situation. Simply put, Satan wants to lie to you to keep you from focusing on what God has for you.

Let me tell you this, once you have been forgiven, you are forgiven! That's it; don't worry about it. Just leave your sin in front of God and walk away from it. God throws it into the sea of forgetfulness, and He doesn't care about it any more. Stop bringing it up! Get over your mistake by coming to terms with your weakness and then keep away from those kinds of situations. Don't mope around, crying that you don't feel the same. Our faith is not by feeling but by believing. Our walk with Christ began with us asking for forgiveness for our sins. We received forgiveness without questions or conditions for all our sins the day we were saved. So isn't the forgiveness then the same forgiveness now? Of course it is! Your sins are no greater now than they were. Sin is sin, my friend. When God forgives you today, it's with the same blood that washed you the first time. Let God forgive you, and then get on with your life.

CHAPTER 7
Giving Your Heart Away

In many relationships, you often notice one person giving more than the other does. One strives harder to make the relationship run smoothly and keep the other person happy—almost as if his or her position in the relationship is to be a giver—or even a servant. Does this describe you?

Don't be confused by what I am trying to explain. (I am not talking about a one-sided dominating relationship.) I'm characterizing a person who is willing to make sacrifices so the relationship will succeed. This person makes a conscious decision to get his or her relationship to a certain place by sacrificing personal needs or wants.

Most of the time, we will put up with a person's bad habits because we love him or her. We want the best for them and believe change is possible. You will see this more in relationships when one of them loves God with all his or her heart and the other isn't as committed or strong in the Lord.

Why are you willing to give more than your share? A person who has a giving nature will probably answer that question this way: "I'd rather suffer myself than watch them suffer."

Why does it seem so natural—like a reflex—for you to give of yourself?
One answer is because your heart has a unique quality. Deep down you have a reservoir of love that God has given you. That love, when tapped, can produce great compassion beyond your understanding. That deep reservoir is natural when you have a strong commitment to Jesus. Why? We are made in His image. His love for us is strong; He can love those who hate Him. He is driven by a deep passion for the lost. The more like Christ you are, the more easily and naturally you will sacrifice for others. You will begin to have a genuine concern for others. The word that best describes this is altruism—the unselfish concern for the welfare of

others. In fact, a recent study showed that marriages with altruistic relationships were happier because each person wanted the best for the other. You might say, "Well, that works for them, but I am the only one who gives in my situation." Well, my friend, don't you worry. God is able.

God can use you to effect change
To some, it may look like you're more of a victim than an instrument. You may feel that way too. In reality, you are God's instrument of change for this person who takes more than he or she gives. Only when you stop feeling like a victim and start feeling like an instrument will God use you!

In Psalms 17:15 the psalmist writes: "As for me, I will behold thy face in righteousness: I shall be satisfied, when I awake, with thy likeness." When David wrote this, he was praying for deliverance from his enemies. He knew obtaining deliverance would mean being devoted to God completely without hindrance. "Awaking in his likeness" symbolizes this heart attitude. The first image you see in the mirror when you get up in the morning should be God's likeness. I think getting out of bed knowing what the day will bring is tough for most people. We all know our schedules and are aware of problems before we fall asleep. When you know you will wake up to a problem, wouldn't it be great to have God's likeness all over you? Imagine facing the day with God's responses instead of yours. When you become totally immersed in Him, you will begin to be used as an instrument to change your loved one for the better. Totally immersed begins when you stop complaining about the relationship to your friends. It also means not starting fights because you're frustrated about giving so much. These attitudes will brew hate and hurt for both of you.

In the study about altruistic relationships, it also showed most religions teach giving of one's self to further relationships. So despite what religious beliefs you might have that are different from mine, one precept holds true in almost all religions: we need to give of ourselves in our relationships to make them better.

I believe you're not giving in vain! Your efforts are not in vain! Before people can give of themselves, they must first love or care about the one to whom they are giving. Do you feel yourself giving in to your compassion? Do you feel your heart is overwhelmed with love? Is your first response to love? Then you're becoming more Christ-like, my friend. I know right now that you may not be seeing the changes you are hoping for in the relationship. Don't worry about what everyone else is saying. Only you two live in your marriage or relationship. No one else knows what you carry or walk through each day. They see from the outside looking in while you're living on the inside trying to build a better outside for the both of you.

Do you want to see happier days for this relationship? Do you sense there could be greatness in store for the two of you? Then don't give up on what you have invested physically, emotionally, and spiritually in your relationship. Trust that you are doing the right thing. Believe God can change your partner. Your stronger, better relationship will give glory to God.

CHAPTER 8
Mind Tricks

Some of the strongest conflicts in relationships are caused by our imaginations. If we leave them to wander on their own, they will take us on an extreme roller coaster ride. I know most of us have wild imaginations. That imagination will attempt to threaten your happiness if you allow it to.

What happens when you see your loved one leave for work? What happens when you have to leave for work? Does your mind begin to wander? Does it begin to tell you that your fiancé has something destructive planned? Are you worried after you leave him? Sometimes we mess things up or complicate our relationships with our overactive minds.

God finally gives you someone special. Instead of being overwhelmed with joy and peace, you feel ravaged with suspicion and jealousy. Why do we always assume the worst? Why do we always feel we are the one being taken advantage of? Maybe you have been hurt in the past. Maybe you are bringing your fears from the past into this new relationship. The truth is, if you cannot trust those who are in your life now, you will never be happy. No matter who is in your life, you need to trust and believe that they have your best interests in mind.

Just your imagination
You also need to trust God. If He put this person in your life, then He has a plan. A good plan. A fair plan in which no one is being taken advantage of. But if you continue to give in to your imagination, you will miss out on this plan. Staying in a relationship with someone who is paranoid is hard! The paranoia makes it difficult to breathe. Every little move is watched or speculated over. Paranoid people sweat the small stuff. Phone calls from friends become suspicious. Lunches with friends become dates. They stress over life's minutia.

Why? Because we tend to get paranoid over what we can't control. Paranoia births fear. Fear grasps our consciousness, showing us only what freaks us out. We even see friends and family as obstacles or threats. We begin to think they are against us or trying to keep the relationship from happening. We get jealous over other people who may have an existing close friendship with our loved one.

Suspicion torments your heart

I think the hardest part of being paranoid is being labeled as insecure. This word will come up when you ask questions—legitimate or not. You will feel it hit you and can't keep your mind from wondering if all is good in your relationship. The worst part is when they say, "You're so insecure." You deny it, but you know it's true. Deep down inside there is a part of you that knows you can't keep yourself from worrying. What's wrong with you? Do you really have the one whom God sent you? Why do you treat him or her so suspiciously?

Facing your fear of allowing a person to have his or her own will is difficult. It might mean you won't be a part of his or her future. You must trust God to keep you together if it's meant to be. No matter what you try to do, your own abilities will not hold this relationship together. If this person is going to leave, that's what's going to happen—either now or in the near future. You can't keep someone in your life who doesn't want to be there. He or she will be miserable if it isn't meant to be—especially if you can sense a parting and overreact because of your insecurity. I know, you can't help yourself. The paranoia is constantly in your thoughts. The slightest inkling of life without him or her is unbearable. What are you to do? Why are you like this?

Claim God's promises

I believe the Bible can help you understand some of those questions. "Casting down imaginations, and every high thing that exalteth itself against the knowledge of God, and bringing into captivity every thought to the obedience of Christ" (2 Corinthians 10:5).

The Word of God says that we will have, at times, ideas, or thoughts that try to sway us from His will. We need to be spiritually armed and ready to combat such destructive foes. We can't sit idle and accept these thoughts as if they are from God. Not every thought is from God. The enemy knows how to tempt you. He will press all your buttons to make you see truth in a lie. We must know God's Word. Only by knowing the Word of God can we understand His promises and will for us. Every time an idea comes up that makes you want to freak out, you need to capture that thought by rebuking it. Satan is the only one coming to your door with accusations. If you accept these accusations, he will keep bringing them. You need to rebuke him now. Stop the trend. Change your outlook. Refuse to let the enemy torment your mind. These mental temptations can be dealt with through faith in God's Word and faith in Him. You need to stand on the Word of God, which says you are blessed. Remember God has brought you this person to love you—not just for you to pour all your love into him or her without receiving any love in return. So trust that the love you are receiving is real.

Thousands of us stare into the eyes of our loved ones every day. We decide in those moments to love and trust them. My friends, you have a choice every day to allow yourself to ruin your relationship or not. Trust God that your loved one is in love with you. Be everything for that person. Be all the love, forgiveness, trust, and respect she or he humanly needs. Believe that no matter what happens, God will give you strength to deal with anything that comes against your relationship. And after you have done all you can, wait. Let God do what He needs to do in you, and then in your loved one. Be the prayer warrior and pillar of faith in your relationship. I think praying is the hardest thing to do when your mind is clouded with paranoia and insecurity. The enemy knows this, so he continues to hit your mind with accusations.

Don't fear! God has your back. Isaiah 35:4 reads: "Say to them that are of a fearful heart, Be strong, fear not: behold, your

God will come with vengeance, even God with a recompense; he will come and save you."

CHAPTER 9
Waking Up

Have you been making wrong choices? Have you ever been involved in the activities of wrong choices? You might not have initiated the bad decision, but you remained faithful to the relationship and participated fully. You never stopped doing what was wrong, no matter how bad you felt. Even though all your instincts, gut feelings, intuition, and spiritual beepers were going off, you stayed.

Have you ever stopped to say, "Not this again." Have you ever known you were going to lose before you started? Or that the plan just didn't seem right, but you stuck with it? Sometimes our loyalty and commitment can lead to trouble, or even our own hurt.

People tend to tolerate someone else's shortcomings because they are in love with him or her. This tolerance may have led to decisions they knew to be wrong, like associating with the wrong people just to keep the other person happy in the relationship. Allowing yourself to drink, or tolerating your partner's drinking or drug use when you know that it will lead to a destructive behavior or addiction is not love. Are you living a life of partying or clubbing just to remain interesting to someone? This tolerance is going to lead to your own destruction if you don't wake up.

Dysfunctional father and loving son
In 1 Samuel 14:24-33 we read of two individuals, Jonathan and his father, Saul. Both men were on a journey together. Saul was the one making the decisions to walk this way, to fight in battles, and to fast. He insisted his men fast until all the battles were over and the victories won for the Lord. Saul was making bad choices. He was caught in a spiritual spiral that was out of control. He was taking his men and his son down with him. Saul couldn't hear God anymore. He longed for His presence, but couldn't feel it. He thought he should fast to please God and to show his men he was a spiritual leader, despite the rumors to the contrary. But nothing

could fill his void. In Saul's mind, winning battles showed God's favor and he needed to assure himself and his kingdom that God was still with them.

All that Saul was responsible for and cared for was at risk. Saul was out of order with God and raged on destructively. Sounds a lot like our relationships, doesn't it?

Imagine thousands of people following a person consumed with paranoia, irrational thinking, and fear. Destruction and chaos will follow in his wake. Relationships so often seem to turn out like this: one person following another because he or she feels tied by a false sense of loyalty or security—or even by force. You have to be careful who you commit yourself to in life. Saul was a hurting individual lost in an emotional struggle that sent him on a destructive journey. People who are hurting will hurt you! Don't get so close and so attached that you can't see how you are being destroyed.

The closest person to Saul at the time of his torrential collapse was his son Jonathan. He was committed to his father emotionally, mentally and physically. He followed him from battle to battle, observing his father's rampages and desperation. He could see the toll these decisions were taking, not only his father, but on him and the entire nation. The men following Saul were so tired they were about to pass out on the road.

Has a relationship ever left you so tired that you felt like passing out? Have you ever felt so starved that your physical body wanted to quit? Jonathan was at that point! Even though he didn't know of his father's decree (or threat) that none should eat until the evening or they would be cursed, he was nevertheless subject to the power of Saul's authority. Now get this—his body needed to eat. It yearned for something to nourish it in the heat of battle. He needed refreshment!

God provided for Jonathan in an amazing way. Without consciously trying to find food, it came to him to taste. God provided what he needed to fix all his aches.

Has a relationship ever left you needing a break from the battles, a break from the worries, the confrontations, the lost sleep, and the heartaches? God knows your situation. He knows your needs. He sees your aches. He wants to help you.

Jonathan was blessed and was about to be blessing to those around him. He tasted just a little bit of the honeycomb offered to him in verse 27 when his eyes were enlightened. Enlightened means "eyes being opened" —or he just woke up! He could now see the situation for what it was. The relationship with his father was similar to any other relationship that has been led with demands, pressure, ultimatums, manipulation, violence, and lies. He could now see the oppression. It's amazing how clear you can see when your eyes have been enlightened. How many times do we tell people what's happening in their lives, and they still don't listen? We even tell them what they need to do to change the situation or how to get out of it, yet they still don't listen. How many times do we refuse to listen? Years may pass and we stay on this journey of battle after battle, and we are still fasting. We are starving and hurting. Our bodies are aching for some nourishment. Yet because we are not reaching out for the provision God has placed in front of us, we continue to starve. We need to wake up!

Look what eventually happened. The men of Israel finally cracked. They had just finished defeating the Philistines. As we read in verse 32, "And the people flew upon the spoil, and took sheep, and oxen, and calves, and slew them on the ground: and the people did eat them with the blood." They were so hungry that they ignored the law against eating meat with blood in it. They couldn't wait to follow the right procedure for preparing their meals, so they just start slamming it down. In other words, this mandate to fast plus their weak emotional states caused them to break the law—to sin.

Emotional ties in relationships also get tiresome. Outbursts and irrational thinking profit no one. You need to look at your life and see what's happening around you. Jonathan didn't sin, because his eyes were opened. He was able to see the distressful situation for what it was. How many of us can say we see the need for change? So if you get that opportunity, cease doing wrong. Make the needed change for you and your loved one. Don't be the person being led around from battle to battle. Be the person who stands up and says: "This is wrong!"

CHAPTER 10
Time to Go

I read an article recently about a scientist who conducted a study on the "inner alarm clock" in human beings. He proved man had an internal alarm clock by asking the individuals in his study to wake up at specific times without an aide of a physical alarm clock or even a clock in the room. These case studies showed that on average, the subjects awoke on time or within fifteen minutes of the time they were told to wake up. Fortunately for alarm clock makers, there is a whole world of us who needs a baseball bat to get us out of bed in the morning. But waking up is not the only inner alarm we have. Scientists have conducted studies on twins who know when the other is in trouble or sensing pain. Women, especially mothers, have long been associated with the infamous "sixth sense"—knowing when something is going wrong with their kids.

Humankind has long been on the mission to prove such alarm systems exist. This inner alarm system theory is not too far-fetched. We can observe animals leaving areas when they sense a natural disaster coming. Therefore, it is quite possible God has installed something in our hearts that senses trouble. In fact, as Christians we experience warnings and guidance by the Holy Spirit when we are sensitive to His voice.

Listen to your heart
I believe God allows us to sense when it's time to move on from a relationship. I believe an inner warning tugs at our hearts and minds, encouraging us to get out when we are not with the person God planned for us.

People are often stuck in bad relationships but don't know how bad it really is or how bad it's going to get. What would you call a bad relationship? What would you call a good one? I think the most successful relationship is based on something transparent. You can't see it—it's more a feeling. To sum it up in one word, it's a "connection." You can't explain it, but you surely know couples who have been together for fifty-plus years and they still seem happy. It's because they have a connection. They took the time to build a loving relationship by fostering the value of mutual respect for one another. They also learned to generally enjoy being with each other. Their spouse is not a burden. They want to spend time together. I believe a successful relationship requires genuine appreciation of one other. Really! If you truly appreciate someone, you treat him or her better. If you care for them as you say you do, then you wouldn't be so quick to cause embarrassment, disrespect, negative thoughts and wishes, or demeaning opinions. True appreciation comes from the heart. Therefore, if you outwardly criticize and mock your partner, your heart doesn't truly appreciate him or her.

Don't get me wrong. You can love a person but not fully appreciate him or her. You simply love at your level, not God's level. We need to love at God's level because it is unconditional and requires nothing in return. His love is freely given and available to everyone. It's merciful and forgiving, not overbearing and controlling.

Many of us hear our inner alarm go off, but choose to ignore it. Sometimes we ignore it because we have pulled someone into our lives who we know is not healthy for us, physically or spiritually. We don't want to give up on a relationship because of some hope we see in the future. We believe if this wrong person would just change, all will be okay, and everything will work out. The longer we ignore the alarm the harder it is to let go, but in our minds, we see ourselves as a couple forever. We continue to tell ourselves that everything depends on this relationship. The sun will not rise and the earth will not revolve if this person is not with us. Deep down in our hearts, however, we know God has a different plan or someone else in mind.

Why can't you walk away? Why does it hurt so badly when you try? Why does it mean so much to keep this person in your life? Because you have allowed yourself to give all of your heart to someone who is not supposed to have it. After all the tears have been cried out and you begin to feel numb from the pain, it's time for you to get up. Get up and know our God has made someone especially for you—someone who is meant to have your heart. In your loneliness and despair, you pulled someone else into that spot.

Warning bells
How can you know if you are hearing the alarm to go? All you need to do is recognize some obvious signs that it's time to move on.

Control is a form of power that one person has over another. It's usually the first sign and the most obvious. Whenever someone tries to manipulate you to his or her desires, you're headed for trouble. When another person is controlling you, it's because you have given him or her power to do so. Anytime someone tells you that you can't go visit your family or friends, and you don't go, you have given away your power to control your decisions. Anytime a person monitors your phone calls or e-mails, it's because you gave them that power. You might notice your partner seems disturbed or uncomfortable when you're around family or friends. This is because they lose a little control over you when you are in a group that cares for you. If this sounds like you, then you are the only person who can change your situation. Your family and friends can help, but cannot do it for you. You need to realize its time to go.

Sexual Sin is what it is, and it's probably the main reason most Christians are in limbo waiting for the right person. Why? Because sexual sin is difficult to stop once it gets started. Either you have to stay away from each other or you have to get married. Sexual sin gives way to depression via guilt. Sexual sin also holds promising relationships back by planting seeds of condemnation and doubt about each other. The shared sexual sin ironically makes a future husband or wife less comfortable about marrying that person, because deep inside they want a man or woman of God who would be stronger for them and refrain from sin.

In 1 Corinthians 6:19 we read, "What? know ye not that your body is the temple of the Holy Ghost which is in you, which ye have of God, and ye are not your own?" So, when someone says sex is part of the relationship or that it's okay because "we will get married later," watch out! That's not what God says. You can't really believe having sex before marriage and then expecting the best for the relationship is realistic, can you? Don't be pressured into having sex because you need to prove something or keep someone happy. These demands should tell you right off the bat that the relationship is not from God.

If you know the pressure is not from your partner, but a desire of your own, then you need some honest self-examination. Do you want to marry this person? If so then start planning the wedding. Don't be surprised if the other person jumps ship. If not, then you need to stop playing house with someone else's promised soul mate.

Threats are bullying tactics practiced by scared people. Whenever a person challenges your will with an ultimatum that he or she will leave if you don't do thus and so, then it's time to go. God is never in a relationship that forces choices with threats. Usually, a person uses threats when he or she feels the loss of control or when the person they want to control isn't listening anymore.

Remember, the Holy Spirit is a gentleman. He waits for your choice to let Him be a part of your daily life. God doesn't threaten us. He speaks with love and compassion to us. He doesn't talk down to you or tell you it's over if you don't do what He says. People will always listen to threats if they are afraid of losing something. Don't be afraid of anything.

Adapting is forcing someone to change his or her lifestyle, culture, beliefs, etc. to "fit" in the relationship. If you have to give up who you are to make this whole thing work, something is wrong. If your longevity in the relationship depends on radically altering your appearance or dress, then you are with the wrong person. If you can't hang out with church folks or Christian friends anymore, then you're headed for trouble. A person who is from

God will want to flow with you in your life. He or she wouldn't want to create changes and block your fellowship with others. A person from God will do his or her best not to interrupt your lifestyle, because he or she wants to be a part of your life—not consume it.

Desperation usually occurs when one person in the relationship is coming to his or her senses and wants out. Remember, you can't hold together something God is pulling apart. No matter how many times your partner tells you "you are mine and nobody else will take care of you," God has plans for you. Even when he or she pulls silly stunts while trying to keep you, like crying, tantrum fits, destroying property and lying, do not be dissuaded. This desperate person knows you are serious, and he or she will pull out all the stops to keep you. Remember, desperate people will do anything to get what they want. They will have no thought or care for what's best for you. They want to keep you, no matter the cost.

Fear is a symptom of someone who is obsessed with the idea of losing you to someone else. Fear walks hand-in-hand with insecurity. We covered some of this earlier in the book, but just to recap, this kind of fear will cause anxiousness and paranoia to overtake the natural place of peace and love. God's relationships don't cause you to cry all night, worrying about losing your beloved. In 1 John 4:18 we learn that "There is no fear in love; but perfect love casteth out fear: because fear hath torment. He that feareth is not made perfect in love." Therefore, if your love is made perfect in Christ, then fear should be obsolete. If you see yourself spending more time aching then rejoicing, it's time to go.

Discouragement, our final but most lethal point, is found in almost every relationship gone bad. Unhappiness and lack of joy is not what God wants in your life. If you are in a relationship with someone who constantly discourages you, it's time to move on. Nobody wants to wake up every morning to a day full of disappointment, but so many of us do. I'm saddened to see the many people who repeatedly decide to walk back into a relationship they know will hurt them. Does God bring you someone who will hurt you? No. Does God tell you to stick in an abusive relationship? No. Does He tell you to try to work it out? Yes. But when the other person does not want to seek help and you're in danger of being abused mentally or physically, it's time to go. You can take only so many years of discouragement, bad treatment, and unfruitful anticipation before you need to be honest with yourself. Did God keep you in this relationship or did you?

Many of you will continue to ignore these signs in your relationship, even after we just covered them. You will say, "That's not what my relationship is like." But the truth is, you have created an idol. You live to love and be with someone who is toxic to you. No matter what, you will stick, even knowing that by doing this you are going against what God has ordained. It comes down to this: your man (or your woman) is your God. Remember that the Bible commands in Exodus 20:5 "Thou shalt not bow down thyself to them, nor serve them: for I the Lord thy God am a jealous God."

My friends, don't make God have to draw a line in the sand for you to decide whom to follow. Don't you want the best from God? Don't you want the right person from God? Oh, you say you got a word from the Lord that this person was for you. Well, maybe you did. Nevertheless, down the road something happened to overturn God's good intentions for you. Maybe this person wasn't ready for marriage. Maybe he or she isn't spiritually mature enough to make a lifetime commitment. Something changed, and now the relationship isn't right. Whatever God's reasons are, know He does have a plan for you. He wants you to have what you need in a spouse. But it may require that you listen more carefully to your inner alarm clock to make it happen.

CHAPTER 11
Ugly Ducklings

Most people know the story of the ugly duckling. A mother duck hatches a large egg and soon discovers the "duckling" is different from everyone else. He becomes an outcast among his family and barnyard friends. He is never happy because he feels inadequate and ugly—inferior to his duckling peers. When he looks in the mirror of the pond, he sees that he does not fit in.

In fact, before he stepped out each morning, he had made up his mind that he was different and didn't belong. His mindset was what I call "the ugly duckling syndrome." No matter how much positive thinking he applied, it would all come crashing down because of what he saw as he looked at his reflection. He assumed others saw only what he saw and believed to be true.

If you remember the story, the duckling was harassed wherever he went. He was wounded and scared emotionally, and nearly froze to death in an icy pond because no one would take him in.

Nobody's perfect
Many of us have negative impressions concerning something small or inferior about ourselves. That's pretty normal. Nobody's perfect. You may be unhappy with something about your appearance. Perhaps your education or your childhood neighborhood was substandard. It's okay to feel a little different or to shy away from others on occasion. But when we allow our small imperfections to get in the way of our relationship happiness, we have a problem. Many of us may never walk into a relationship because of our fear of being inferior or less qualified. God may have the perfect person just for you, yet you don't accept him or her because you can't accept yourself.

Let me give you some distinguishing attributes of someone who may feel like he or she is an ugly duckling.

- You wake up every morning wondering why you were born different. You question God about your existence.

- You become jealous of those whom are compared to you. If a sibling is involved, a rivalry is born.

- You feel awkward when surrounded by successful or attractive people.

- You seem more sensitive to criticism than others are.

- You may give up easily because you never seem to win. You find it easy to give up because you're tired of losing— so tired that you don't even try in relationships or even friendships.

- When troubles begin to hit, you automatically count your losses then move on. Why? Because in your mind, it is easier to lose then to get hurt again. God may want you to stick it out. But every time you see familiar signs of defeat, you bail out.

- You don't think anyone will want you. After all the rejection and abuse in the past, you feel less adequate. You tend to let your failures or mistakes create an image that you are "less" of a person. When something good comes along, you talk your way out of it with words like: "You deserve someone better" or "I am not everything you need." Why? You have allowed your failures to determine your future. The devil wants you to feel different to separate yourself from others and feel abandoned. The Bible says in 1 Peter 5:8 "Be sober, be vigilant; because your adversary the devil, as a roaring lion, walketh about, seeking whom he may devour." He is out there my friends trying to destroy you! If he can make you destroy yourself by not allowing people in, he wins!

- You may have unintentionally built a wall or barrier around your heart because you always seem to get the short end of the stick. Sometimes it stems from childhood disappointments. You felt you were never the pretty one in the family growing up. You may have never been first in anything or given the first choices. You were compared to your siblings in anything and everything you did. You felt like you were never appreciated for your own achievements or accomplishments. You were never the favorite in your parents' eyes.

God doesn't want you wrapped up in your self-pity or imperfections. He doesn't want you worrying about what you should look like or where you should live. He wants you living life the way He made you to live it. What you call differences He calls uniqueness. He made everybody unique. Plastic surgery can change your outward appearance. You may even feel good about your new look. Nevertheless, plastic surgery will never change years of hurt and torment or years of other people's opinions shaping your future. These people have hurt you, unintentionally or intentionally, and have damaged your ability to receive love. In fact, you have allowed the hurt others caused to keep you from God's will. You have pushed good people away when they tried to love you. You ran away when they wanted to hold you close to their hearts.

God doesn't make junk!
What can you do to break the ugly-duckling mentality? If you are feeling like you're being compared to your sibling, you need to be firm in telling your parents or friends, "I am not my sibling, I am me." Tell yourself that you are a new person in God, not playing second fiddle to anyone!

We must change our attitudes about our life by remembering God has no ugly ducklings. Remember the Word of

69

God tells you in Romans 8:37 that we are "more then conquerors." Don't accept being labeled an outcast! No matter how easy it is to allow yourself to feel defeated, don't give up on relationships prematurely.

Know that you *will* be part of someone's life. God has not cursed you! He has a plan, and even through your grief, you will be a blessing to many.

Stop whining!
Although there are valid reasons for many emotional dysfunctions due to being branded an ugly duckling, far too many of life's so-called ugly ducklings have taken advantage of the situation. You see these folks on television talk shows and reality shows screaming at their parents or beating up their siblings in front of a live audience. Throughout the overly dramatic interviews, we may hear a couple of sincere words, but most of it will be drowned out by the constant cries of "not fair" or the screams of "why me?" Sadly, it isn't fair. Are these "ugly ducklings" to blame because they were born different? Are they able to change themselves instantly to our satisfactions and specifications?

No, they can't, at least not overnight. The most important thing that must change is *attitude.* A person must rise above his or her childhood horrors or physical ailments by purposely believing he or she is not an ugly ducking. No matter the trauma, God gives new life.

Remember, God has planned the best for you. Happiness is not about your clothing, money, friends, cars, homes, or stature. Your outward appearance will not bring you lasting joy. Do your best to fight the naysayers. Make sure you believe with confidence that the Word of God is true for you. Search the Scriptures to learn what God says about you.

The ugly duckling eventually turned into a beautiful swanand was the talk of the pond. The years of perseverance built into him the character needed for success. You too will continue to grow into the beauty God has designed for your life. The years that have been full of hurt, lack, or sadness have built a stronger, loving, and more understanding person, whom God can use for His glory.

CHAPTER 12
When It's Over—Destiny or Destruction?

I believe most of us would agree that planning to marry someone and then not marrying him or her is a hard pill to swallow. After praying about the decision to marry and telling everyone you know you're sure, it's torture to realize it's not going to happen. Your soon-to-be husband or wife is calling it off.

Many times, we want to hold a person in our life no matter what may be going wrong. We want them even more than life itself. Even though being together begins to tear us apart emotionally and physically, we still won't let it go.

Love hurts!
Have you ever prayed so much for someone you loved that it hurt? I mean, so much that your body literally ached? My friends, you can put in prayer time about your relationship until it becomes all you ever pray about. You can spend hours, even days, crying out to God to help you. Nothing seems to change. After all the hours you prayed, has God not answered? Why? Why does every day in this relationship seem like a rollercoaster? Why do you feel like you're close to having everything you ever wanted, then in a matter of hours it's upside down again? How long will you continue to go through this?

All of this high drama becomes a drain and a strain on any relationship. In any relationship that runs hot and cold, one of the parties will eventually say enough is enough. He or she will leave the relationship, believing it's better for all concerned. But what happened? Why did she leave you? Why couldn't he see your love for him? Why would he think you would be okay without him? Didn't she love you? Didn't she know you couldn't live without her?

But, now you're alone, and everything hits you. It hurts. Your head is hanging. Nobody you talk to understands. You keep questioning God. You begin to wonder why you received all the go-ahead signs.

You know you heard all the confirmations correctly. Even prayer partners gave you thumbs up. So why are you now alone, crying bitter tears? Nothing makes sense!

You keep trying to reconnect with the person who left you, but this time it's different. You feel the difference—it almost feels like this could be permanent. You want to scream when you realize your beloved is actually gone! You feel so alone. Nothing you do is helping the situation. Tactics that worked in the past are no longer effective. No matter what you try, you can't put it back together. If finally begins to sink in that this person is gone for good. You're a mess and in shambles. You can't seem to focus on anything but your loss and your misery.

After about two or three weeks, you're still crying. Months pass while you sit on your couch and mourn over him or her. Not a day goes by that you can't stop thinking about the failed relationship, and what could have been. Eventually you hit rock bottom. After not returning calls, avoiding church, skipping outings, and staying away from friends and family—after all the tears, after all the prayers, and after all the worrying—what do you need to do?

Remember, God is in control of your life, even your romance. Sometimes He wants to place someone in your life. He may have chosen this particular person for you. But just like with salvation, marriage is a person's free choice. Each one of us needs to be equipped mentally, spiritually, and physically to handle the route God has for us. If someone isn't willing to go forward, that is his or her choice. God will never force anyone to be with someone. You don't want someone who has to convince himself or herself to be with you. It's not fun! He or she will always second-guess you and the decision to be with you.

When the smoke clears, you need to stand up, wash your face, and dust yourself off. That's right. You need to pull yourself together and know God hears your prayers and feels your pain.

How a king grieves

Let's look again in 2 Samuel. In chapter 12:13-23. King David had been praying and fasting for the life of his critically ill newborn son. He cried out to God night and day for several days. He knew his son would die, because of what the prophet Nathan told him. But he kept holding on, crying and screaming for God to change His mind. Then one night as he was praying, he saw his servants whispering in the corner. They were afraid to tell him his son had, in fact, died. They perceived he wouldn't be able to handle the news since he had cried for days while his child was alive. How much more will he hurt now? David realized as they whispered that his son had died. He asked them about it, and they told him the news. But to their astonishment, David didn't fall apart.

We read in 2 Samuel 12:20-23: "Then David arose from the earth, and washed, and anointed himself, and changed his apparel, and came into the house of the Lord, and worshipped: then he came to his own house; and when he required, they set bread before him, and he did eat. Then said his servants unto him, What thing is this that thou hast done? Thou didst fast and weep for the child, while it was alive; but when the child was dead, thou didst rise and eat bread. And he said, While the child was yet alive, I fasted and wept: for I said, Who can tell whether God will be gracious to me, that the child may live? But now he is dead, wherefore should I fast? Can I bring him back again? I shall go to him, but he shall not return to me."

King David did what we all need to do after we have exhausted our emotions and prayers for someone. He stood up, washed his face, changed his clothes, and accepted God's will. David never cursed God or complained; he just accepted what had happened. He still felt the hurt. After all, his child was dead; but he dealt with it and moved on. God sees your tears and pain. He sees the agony you're living in right now. No matter if a person never changes his or her mind, decides to leave permanently, never becomes your partner, you have to let it go. Pray. Pour out your heart to God, then leave it in His hands and move on.

Danger ahead

What are some of the dangers of not letting go? When you're holding something tightly in your hand, you're preventing God from placing something else in it. You might be praying for someone to stay with you who may not be yours to keep. You may be jealous over someone who is not even yours to get jealous about. You also could be riding an emotional wave of love for a person who doesn't feel the same way for you.

I know I mentioned this before, but love is not one-sided. To succeed in love with someone, you must both have a love that is strong and apparent for one another.

You have the choice to go on living in Destiny or in Destruction. When your relationship with God begins to take a nosedive and your life's focus becomes a person or relationship, you can't discern God's will. To know His will, you must focus on Him and the precepts in His Word.

I believe the hardest thing to do is to let go and give a person you're madly in love with or care so much for over to God. You want to make sure you can guide that person "back" to you. You want to make sure they hear every prophet and every preacher, and read every book on relationships. You think you can fix your beloved, so you make it your mission on earth to get him or her healed emotionally, hoping the two of you will get back together.

My friend, look at your life right now. Are you living your life for God or for your relationship? Look at your life, seriously. Are you always running around trying to satisfy somebody just to keep him or her in your life?

Remember the title of this chapter—Destiny or Destruction. What are you doing? Are you holding someone in your life at all costs? If so, you're headed straight to destruction. However, if you let God have that person, you may finally reach your destiny!

CHAPTER 13
Untouchable

This is the chapter many will pass up, because it will hurt to hear the truth.

I want to discuss what I call the "Untouchable," a person who believes he or she is not held accountable to God for sexual sin. This person feels no guilt or remorse after committing sexual sin. They take God's grace and forgiveness for granted. The truth is, none is exempt from sin. No one is above the law when it comes to sin. Sin affects everyone.

Some people of faith may choose to ignore certain behaviors, but we need to know we will all be held accountable for everything we do here on earth. Sin is a big issue, but no sin seems to bring down more ministers and believers than sexual sin. It has been a problem since the beginning of time. We have been influenced and mesmerized by our fleshly desires and have adapted our decisions about love and sexually accordingly. Don't get me wrong. What I'm talk about here is not just making a mistake in a relationship. What I am addressing is the person who believes sexual sin is allowed in God's Word. I think we have to address this subject honestly.

Many couples today battle the issue of having "to wait." Do you have boundaries or markers for your relationship to keep you in check? Are you being honest in the relationship? God has designed you as a gift to another person. You also have a gift from God of another person waiting for you. We are accountable to Him as to how we handle every relationship we are involved in.

If you don't watch yourself, you could be swept up into falling in a moment. That moment could have damning repercussions to your marriage and friendships. You could end up spiritually hurting not only yourself, but also the other person. Some people never recover because they feel they let God down in the most ultimate way. Years pass, and they are still crying about their sexual sin!

Flee Temptation

Sin is sin, my friend. You have to ask yourself if you purposely allow yourself to be in compromising positions. Or, do you purposely seek out ways to put another person in compromising positions. Do you openly and intentionally allow yourself or someone you're with to sin against God's Word? Many times, sin in a relationship occurs because we allow ourselves to be alone with someone we shouldn't be alone with. We know our weaknesses and our limits, but foolishness is no excuse for giving in to temptation. Of course, you will give in. You know you will give in. Of course, you will not stop—deep down, you don't want to stop. But self-control is a big part of the Christian walk. So lacking self-control is not good. You always have a choice. You can walk away from a relationship going too far sexually at anytime. Again, you choose to stay in it because deep down you want someone to love you in that way.

Do you think you can sin and not be held accountable? Do you think you're exempt? Do you sit in church knowing that afterward you're going to sin sexually? Remember, God sees all and knows all. No matter whom else you can fool, God knows the truth. If you can still sit in the pew with no remorse for your premeditated sexual misconduct, then I need to share a scripture with you that really drives the point home.

1 John 1:5-10: "This then is the message which we have heard of him, and declare unto you, that God is light, and in him is no darkness at all. **If we say that we have fellowship with him, and walk in darkness, we lie, and do not the truth.** But if we walk in the light, as he is in the light, we have fellowship one with another, and the blood of Jesus Christ his Son cleanseth us from all sin. **If we say that we have no sin, we deceive ourselves, and the truth is not in us.** If we confess our sins, he is faithful and just to forgive us our sins, and to cleanse us from all unrighteousness.

If we say that we have not sinned, we make him a liar, and his word is not in us" (emphases mine).

Those words are self-explanatory, my friend. If you are in intentional sin and do not have a repentant heart, you are in danger of never knowing Christ. God's truth in you must be evident. Somewhere deep down inside, you must feel remorse. If you do, then God will help you change. Just ask Him to allow the Holy Spirit to touch your heart and forgive your foolishness right now. I urge you to open your heart to the truth.

Face the consequences
Here are a few damaging results of sexual sin. Some hit both parties in the relationship, but often the effects are stronger in one person than the other. Some people are more calloused than others are.

- **Depression** begins to take over the mind of the individual.

- **Anxiety attacks** begin to become frequent even shortness of breath.

- **Fear** begins to grasp the mind and surround them all the time.

- **Unforgiveness** doesn't allow the release of past failures.

How can you know if you are in an Untouchable relationship? Here are a few guidelines to help you discover if you are an Untouchable.

- You try to hide your relationship because of sin.

- You are ashamed to be in the house of God.

- You make excuses for your sin.

- You ignore God's rules and warnings.

79

- You purposely look for opportunities to sin.

- The Word of God has no effect on your conscience.

- You manipulate and become angry if you can't get your way.

- You are not receptive to correction.

- You choose to ignore godly advice and counsel.

- You refuse to hearken to the Holy Spirit.

- You look for reasons to validate your choices, even when you know they are wrong, because you want the moment.

We must bring ourselves into obedience to God's Word. You're a Christian, a believer; you're not some star on TV or the movies. This is real life. You may not get a second chance to fix what is wrong in your life today. You are holy—act like it. Live God's lifestyle! Don't pretend to be saved. God loves you no matter what, but don't take His love for granted, my friend!

SECTION 3

THE COMMITMENT OF PARTNERS

CHAPTER 14
Commitment

One of the greatest challenges to overcome in marriage is
familiarity—knowing someone too well and for so long. My
twelve years of marriage seems like a whole bunch to some people.
In reality, it's just a drop in the bucket compared to some
marriages. Think about this for a minute. We have all been to a
wedding reception at some time. During the reception, the DJ will
often have a dance for the married couples in attendance. After the
dancing begins, he starts a countdown of sorts for all the dancers
by politely asking those who have been married five years or less
to leave the dance floor. Then those married ten years or less and
so on and so on, until he reaches forty-five years, then fifty years
(usually the grandparents of the bride or groom). I am always
amazed to see couples who have stayed married for so long. It used
to be common. But today, with divorce statistics going through the
roof, you appreciate it more when you see a couple who has a long
history together.

It's a blessing to have a spouse.
You are blessed to have such a person in your life—someone you
call husband or wife. Many have searched for the right person,
only to remain alone. When you get married, you form a
partnership between the two of you. In your wedding vows, you
make a commitment to each other that is a commitment to pledge
your love to that person forever. This commitment doesn't mean
just during the blessed times. Neither does it mean when you feel
like it. It means no matter what happens in life, you are your
spouse's partner through it all.

Your BFF
I recently performed a wedding service for one of my best friends.
I interviewed the beautiful couple, as most ministers would, to get
an idea of their love for one another. The words they spoke of each
other made me think: they are each other's best friend.

Your wife or husband *should* be your best friend. Jesus said in Matthew 19:6: "Wherefore they are no more twain, but one flesh...." In other words, when you said, "I do," you said, "this person is my best friend." Remember, true love will always be tested. It's up to you to keep your spouse in the correct position in your heart.

How? One way is to have a goal of where you want to be together in few years. Then you can see what each of you needs to work on to get to your goal. You also need to make yourself available to the interests and work of your spouse.

Many marriages end up in the graveyard of divorce because neither spouse took an interest in what the other liked or did. So what if you don't like what your spouse enjoys? Learn to like something about it, or at least decide to spend time with your spouse while he or she is involved in it. Be supportive, even if you don't participate.

When time is spent away from each other, whether work, travel or whatever, it will test the love you have between you. For this reason, I recommend you set four standards early in your marriage.

- You will look for encouragement in each other. In other words, you must be the only person your spouse comes to with his or her deepest emotions.

- You must be each other's strength. Look to each other to build up and not tear down.

- You need to be the one from whom your spouse gets his or her joy and laughter.

- You need to be each other's hero. Physical affairs or emotional affairs begin when another person is "there" for your spouse. Men, you need to be the rescuer. Most women will tell you they just want to be rescued. Don't let someone else be in that position. That is your right! Women, your guy wants to be admired. Don't let the women at the office step into your place in this crucial area. Make sure your man knows he is recognized and appreciated for everything he does.

I have been asked what I thought was the secret to having a successful marriage. A few answers pop up in my mind right away. Communication, honesty, respect, and love are all important. But I think commitment is the most important. It takes two people totally committed to one another to succeed. No matter the victories or defeats, if two people are committed to each other, they will make it.

Material things can be replaced. But a partner who sticks with you through the toughest times is priceless. A partner is a special person that in the deepest part of his or her heart accepts you no matter what. My friends, look at the relationship you have today. Are you committed to this partnership? Are you in for the long haul? Today, purpose to challenge yourself to be committed to your partner like never before.

CHAPTER 15
The Great Compromise

Marriage counselors often encourage couples to compromise to make their relationships more successful. That makes sense. We can't always get what we want; neither can we always make another person happy 100 percent of the time. Happily married couples tell us their success is due to being willing to give sacrificially to each other. There is some truth in that claim. Even close friends tell you that you must put up with pleasing another person at the cost of your own choices at times.

But the larger truth is that in order to compromise, we must first want to be in our relationship 100 percent. Do you really want to be with the person whom you're with right now? Before you can compromise honestly and effectively, a question must be answered. How much are you truly committed to this person and the well-being of the relationship? Answer this for me. What keeps you there? What keeps you with this person? Is it comfort? Is it finances? Is it security? Is it the kids? Be honest with yourself when you answer this. Know that whatever your answer is, only one answer is the acceptable one.

Love is the answer
We can genuinely love almost anyone, but giving all your heart and self to someone must happen only when you have the same love in return. Without this type of love for one another, no compromise in the world will help your marriage. Unless your love for one another is completely focused on one thing—that you want to be with each other no matter what—you will probably have a difficult time dealing with compromises. Without commitment, one or both of you will feel like you're giving more than the other is. You will complain that it's not fair, that you're being taken advantage of all the time. Negative feelings will begin to arise and fights will take place.

Before you said, "I do" there was "I want." You remember the prayers you lost sleep over crying to God. You prayed to God that He would give you a person to love and to have as your partner in life. You waited and waited. Now you have what you asked for but are having problems imagining life with this person for one more week, not to mention forever.

When you were blind with love, you called all his or her hang-ups pet peeves. Now they are nuisances and a wrecking ball on your dream of a happy marriage. Isn't it amazing how much we all tolerate in the beginning of our marriages? We ignore the little annoyances—they barely bother us. We might even have thought the funny habits were charming. But after we have lived a while with the person we prayed for, and know all his or her hang-ups, we pick on them or use them to dilute our passion.

Ephesians 5:28-29 reads, "So ought men to love their wives as their own bodies. He that loveth his wife loveth himself. For no man ever yet hated his own flesh: but nourisheth and cherisheth it, even as the Lord the church." You want the best for yourself, don't you? You would never want to be put through the emotional hell of a bad relationship. Why would you want to put yourself through a living nightmare of jealousy, anger, and mistrust? Why do we allow ourselves to emotionally hurt the one we love?

1 Corinthians 13:8 reads, "Charity never faileth." Everything in this world may come to an end, but love will never fail. That's the simplest translation. You could be at the brink of disaster at home, but your love must be strong enough so that it will never give up.

Why do we set ourselves up to compromise? Why do we feel we have to? I mean, isn't it easier to just get fed up and demand our own way? Absolutely! We shouldn't have to put ourselves on hold all the time. What about him? Can't he ever give in?

When you start responding this way, my friend, God is probably working in you. Sometimes you need to get frustrated before you can realize something is wrong with your attitude.

Sometimes you have to get ticked off and say something you regret before you realize how unloving you have become.

Before He can work a healing in your relationship, God often has to press down to show you where the pain really lies. You must be able to deal with every aspect of your relationship, not just what you find tolerable.

CHAPTER 16
Keeping What You Have

I receive numerous calls, e-mails, and letters asking me the same question repeatedly: How do you change someone you're married to who is not saved? I am amazed at how many believers marry unbelievers.

God doesn't want us to be alone. He wants to give us the desires of our hearts, and a companion is an admirable desire. But many believers think God put this person in their life to help bring him or her to Jesus. Maybe He did, but you should never believe that is a mandate for marrying someone who does not put God first in his or her life.

Missionary or missing out?
If you allow yourself to think you're the reason and way they will come to Jesus, then you are deceived. You will most likely fail. We cannot put our timelines and deadlines on anyone to be saved. Everyone is an individual; we all make individual choices. In my experience, I have seen that the more you make a fuss about salvation, the more the other person will draw away or become reluctant. Eventually, you will focus so much on the other's need for salvation that you will lose focus on your relationship.

Focusing on an unsaved spouse's lack of faith is dangerous because it will begin to plant seeds of doubt about the validity of the marriage relationship. You will begin to think you're stuck— that you have no way out and you made a mistake by getting into this marriage with a nonbeliever. The truth is, when you begin to think you're stuck is usually also the time you are becoming frustrated that he or she hasn't changed. You need to let God change your spouse.

Jesus tells us to let our light so shine before men that we may glorify our Father which is Heaven. We have to live our life toward God. Many of your choices to do something God's way rather than the world's way will be noticed. You don't think so, but

I have found that a spouse who hasn't come to the Lord usually admires the other because of his or her stand. Yes, arguing about tithing, going to church, and fellowshipping with other believers will be challenges to deal with, depending on the unsaved spouse's insecurity and trust level. But your faith will change him when you leave him in God's hands.

Are you in the way of progress?
Admittedly, the situation is hard to endure. The person you're supposed to spend your life with doesn't want your Jesus. Your inner struggle with your spouse is tiresome. Why is it that the person we love the most is the hardest person to change?

We have to look at this differently. Just as doctors don't operate on their own loved ones because of the conflict of interest, and the added stress, we have to know that sometimes we can't be the direct soul winner for our loved one. Many times, I prayed for family members to get saved. At the time, they were too close to me to receive any godly love or instruction. Remember what Paul said in 1 Corinthians 3:6, "I have planted, Apollos watered; but God gave the increase." God will put others around besides you to get the job done. Sometimes we are too close to the situation. We want the change so bad that it frustrates us and makes our relationship tougher than it needs to be. Marriage is a work in progress every day. Adding witnessing to the mix can lead to some volatile moments. Remember, we are transformed by the renewing of the mind. Your spouse's reprobate mind has yet to be transformed. His or her thinking and your thinking will not balance out at all. He or she will insult you, largely regarding your faith. You need to hold on to what you believe. Take your scriptures to the Lord. Take Joshua 24:15, "…but as for me and my house, we will serve the Lord." God is faithful to His Word. Let God do His work without interference and instruction from you.

Paul writes in 1 Corinthians 10:13, "There hath no temptation taken you but such as is common to man: but God is faithful, who will not suffer you to be tempted above that ye are able; but will with the temptation also make a way to escape, that ye may be able to bear it." So you see, my friend, you're not stuck. You're exactly where God has and needs you today. But your outlook needs to be a little different. You may not be seeing the results you want today, but you are being watched by your spouse and by everyone who knows of the situation. Imagine when salvation does finally happen. Your friends, your coworkers, your family will all witness the testimony of your love, patience, and faith. What a wonderful testimony that will be!

CHAPTER 17
Keeping the Romance

After being married to someone for several years, it is easy to become bored with the routine you are in and even with the person to whom you are married. Our minds and emotions easily become disconnected from one another, either by choice or by distraction. Relationships appear better on the "other side." Maybe your mind fantasizes about good times with someone else. You may even entertain acting on the idea, especially when there is flirtation going on. The truth is, the main reason romance becomes dull or dead in our relationships is because we allow it to get to that point.

That lovin' feelin'
Where is the excitement in your relationship at today? Have you allowed your interest to transfer to a coworker or friend? Have you given the romance that belongs to your spouse to another? Romance is more than sex, my friend. Romance is your essence, your conscious being that makes another feel wanted and loved. Romance is what makes your spouse attracted to you. It belongs to him...to her. Romance is the undivided attention that lets your spouse know he or she is the love of your life.

How do we give this attention away? When is a glance more than a glance? When is a hug too personal? When the glance or hug is given with ulterior motives—when you want to hug or have that second glance. When your mind and heart are drifting away from your spouse. If you are at this point, you need to check your heart against your true intentions. Yes, it is easy to fall in love with just about anyone. But should you? Is this person really deserving of your love and admiration? Is he or she stealing your attention from your spouse? Or are you giving it away?

I want to give you some simple points that may help you if you're going through something like this right now.

- Purpose to keep your heart in your marriage. Don't wait until tomorrow to start moving back toward the one you love. Do it today. If you start down the path of sharing your love, you will eventually leave your spouse for another. Sin is too strong and temptation too unbearable to stop. Romance begins in your heart. Keep it interested in your true love. The devil will always make life look greener on the other side. He will make your attraction to another seem like love, but it's not. Be true to your heart and your spouse by telling yourself the truth.

- Don't start to eye those in the office or grocery store who don't belong to you. Most times the most attractive and desirable people will be married. Hello. Don't you think we could see that coming? Of course, the enemy wants take out the happily married couples. That's why God tells us in the Bible not to covet one another's spouse (see Exodus 20:17). Coveting is a deep emotion. If you feed the covetous heart, it will overtake you.

- Third, you must be happy in your current situation. Finding someone else during troubled times at home or even due to lack of attention will confuse your true feelings. The person you find may fill your needs now. He or she may fill all the voids in your marriage perfectly. What about tomorrow? If you get together with that new person, will he or she keep those voids filled, or will you just have different voids? If you have voids in your marriage relationship right now, perhaps you need to search your heart to see if it's you or something else that needs fixing before you add someone new to your life.

Why is it so important to find a way to be happy in your current situation? Isn't it worth trying to keep it together if you were really in love when you got together? Now besides situations of abuse, control and manipulation, and infidelity, married couples should stay together. Try. Try to find contentment with the one you first loved before all the problems started.

96

- Fourth, you can't think of yourself as stuck or trapped. This notion will start your heart yearning for someone else you know presently or knew in the past. We don't need that stuff being stirred up right now, do we? How many times have you thought of someone you once dated or almost married or could have been happy with? If you begin doing that to yourself, you will end up with some crazy thoughts. And those crazy thoughts lead to exploration. You might start Google searching and creating private e-mail addresses to contact someone you shouldn't be contacting. The could've, should've and would've needs to be left outside the door. Remember, anything you feel you need to hide is usually something you shouldn't be doing. Mistrust is the offspring of deception. Deception is the beginning of disloyalty. Disloyalty will often lead to divorce.

CHAPTER 18
Chasing the Challenge

Have you ever had someone in your life who drained you physically and mentally? You felt you had nothing else to give to them or to the relationship. How long have you been waiting for him or her to change?

You're exhausted! Something has to give or you're going to break. If you haven't left already, I bet you're thinking about doing so now. Yes. It might be easy to walk away or drive off with your car packed. But you still have to deal with the emotions that tie you to this person.

In my experience, I've noticed that the highly volatile relationships have the strongest ties. Why? Maybe because anger and hostility are strong emotions just like love and kindness. Negative emotions are like any other emotions—they create a bond. The bond, no matter how bad the emotion, is binding.

We've all known couples who argue all the time, but stay together. People shake their heads, wondering why or how. Outsiders believe these fighting couples would be happier without each other and would find that out if they separated. But, just like love and kindness can build a lasting relationship, anger and hostility can build one too, but always at the expense of joy, peace, and common sense.

Enough already!
What if you have given it your all and see no change? You are finally fed up— completely. You don't even want to go home. I mean, you're in your car after work or leaving the grocery store and you just can't bear the idea of driving home to him…to her. You're going to argue. Accusations will fly. Your heart can't take any more pain. You want to keep this person in your life, but at what expense? Is your mental and physical health worth it? How many times do you need to visit your doctor over anxiety attacks or heart failure?

Does an ambulance need to pull up in your driveway for everybody to get the hint about what's going on? Aren't you tired of all the run around?

Many of us will pursue jobs, careers, or even friendships to the extreme. We will sacrifice and hang on until we get what we want. No matter what others think or what it takes, we stick with it and wait. Do we wait with the same expectation and determination when it comes to chasing and then keeping our love?

You can't give up on your spouse! Even if you are the only one pulling, trying, working, praying, you have to keep yourself in the race. Don't bail out. Where is the desire you once had to pursue your love? Ask yourself this crucial question, and give an honest answer: How much do you love your spouse? Is there enough love left to change your relationship for the better?

In Galatians 6:9 Paul writes, "And let us not be weary in well doing: for in due season we shall reap, if we faint not." How many years have you put into your marriage? Believe God will answer your prayers. You must keep pursuing good for each other. You have to want God to do great things with your relationship. Tiredness and frustration is flesh. Dig deep into the spiritual person God has created you to be. Don't let the flesh dictate your relationship growth. Waiting for change in someone you love is hard. The greatest challenge is not walking out on what you have devoted the better part of your life to. Believe God no matter what others tell you. If you really believe that God wants you to work your relationship out, and there is no abuse, then stick with it until it changes. Sometimes it may take letting the person go for a while so God can deal with him or her.

CHAPTER 19
Our Returnable Society

We have been born into a returnable society. In most shops in America, purchases can be returned within thirty days with a receipt. Wal-Mart, for instance, will even give you a gift card or "in-store credit" if you don't have a receipt. This makes it easy for anyone to take back what he or she doesn't want.

Sometimes when a relationship turns frustrating, we mistake the troubles as a sign that God wants us to get out of it. We want to return it for a newer, more user-friendly version! Instead, we need to look at troubles as a sign that it's time to grow. You should be able to look back on your relationship with no regrets, knowing that after all is said and done, you did everything possible to make it work out. You can't take back what God has given you. You prayed and cried for this person in your life. You want this person to stay in your life or you wouldn't be reading this book. But I have no secret formula for how to change your spouse, and there is no answer as to when you can expect him or her to "come around."

What about you?
Many problems in relationships stem from selfishness and immaturity. Step back and honestly look at your situation for a minute. Ninety-nine percent of your battles, arguments, and disagreements come from selfishness or wanting more attention than your spouse gives you. It's a natural reaction in any relationship. One party needs the security, the other the affirmation. Usually women need the security of care and men need affirmation that they are appreciated.

Thousands of people today sit in their home asking God why they are in their current relationship. They ask God why He allows them to be tormented with all their perceived problems. Everything is clouded by their "Doomsday" attitude. Sometimes God will allow you to get so frustrated that you want to scream. You can't handle this anymore!

This often occurs because He needs you to get mad enough at the situation to be able to let go of it. Only then can He can step in to do the work.

Hold on

You can't give up on better days. You must hold on to the promise. My favorite scripture in the whole Bible is Hebrews 13:5, "Let your conversation be without covetousness; and be content with such things as ye have: for he hath said, I WILL NEVER LEAVE THEE, NOR FORSAKE THEE" (emphasis mine). Trust in God. No matter what others may tell you or how much they make fun of your situation, you will have the last laugh. The great thing about God's plan is that in His power, we will make it. He knows what you are made of because He made you. He knows what a fighter and survivor you really are.

We expect a miracle to change our situation. God is able to do this, of course. He can. He is God! But how do you respond when a miracle doesn't happen? You're still living in the same situation and with the same problems. What can you do? You do what God expects you to do. You do what the Word of God tells you to do. You allow God time to work in your situation, because sometimes it's not the other person God is working on—it's you. You're the one who needs a little tinkering. Have faith that you're not in a hopeless situation. Believe He will change your situation. Trust that God is doing all that is needed for this moment in your life. Tonight before you get into your prayer closet to ask for God for help, know your spouse isn't returnable. Ask God where change can take place in you as well.

CHAPTER 20
Past Loves

Many of you may fit into this scenario: you have someone tucked away in the back of your mind who means something special to you—someone who meant a lot to you years ago. Every now and then, you pause for a few minutes to wonder him or her. Where is he? What is he doing now? Is she happy? Did she ever get married? Does she wonder about me? These questions are just a few that may flit across your mind. You may be in a relationship with someone whom you're madly in love with today. You're happy with whom you chose to spend the rest of your life building a family. You may enjoy every part of your life to this point. So why do you think of that long-ago person? Why does he or she just pop up in your mind from time to time? Why are you still interested in his or her well-being?

Are these thoughts wrong? Is this fair to your current relationship? Should you feel a bit guilty? All these questions have different answers for different people and situations. So before I give you those answers, let me ask a question. Why does this person haunt you? Why is he or she imprinted into the back of your mind? Why, after all these years, do you still care? I believe because at one time your love was pure, uncontaminated, and untainted by life. You genuinely loved him or her with all your heart. You may have even planned a future together at one time. This person was to be the one with whom you expected to spend the rest of your life.

Always on my mind...
Do memories of that old flame flare up when you are doing something or about to do something you thought you would be doing with him or her? Maybe you're about to have a baby. Maybe you're reaching a certain age you expected to be with him or her. Maybe you just took a vacation to an exotic place. Or you could be buying your first house. Whatever it is, you always thought you would be with this other person at this point in your life. These are

a few reasons he or she stays on your mind. To put it simply, you still daydream about having a life with your "first love." That's why this image seems stapled onto your forehead at certain times.

You should feel guilty only if you do something to evolve your daydream to reality. If you try to hunt down this person to set up a secret rendezvous, you have a problem. Any innocent meeting can result in an opportunity to have an affair. Any time you act out a fantasy or dream outside your marriage, it becomes a sin. Your loyalty belongs to your spouse, unconditionally. Simply put, God doesn't share us with any other; why should our spouse have to? You are one with your spouse no matter who comes back from the past. No matter what you shared with your old flame, it's in the past. No matter how familiar you were with that person, it's still the past.

No matter what you do to not think about this person, it will be impossible to stop. He or she will always be in the back of your mind. That's okay! As long as you keep your past loves there—in the past.

Don't feel guilty

As long as you keep your past love in the back of your mind and don't try to build a romance with him or her, you can be guilt free. At one time, this person meant the world to you, so it's natural to have a general concern. Remember to keep the concern in its place *at all times.* Know where you're at today. They enemy wants you to be tempted. Wondering is natural, but don't try to insert this person into your spouse's place. The fantasy always looks better than reality. And the reality is, that old relationship didn't work out.

Yes. You may have been in love. Something about that person was extra special and touched your heart. Deep down, you have a spot for them that won't easily go away. But eventually, my friend, you need to let it go.

CHAPTER 21
The Nature of Relationships

Many of us walk through the malls during busy Christmas-week hours searching for gifts for family and friends. After hearing "Is this for someone special" for the third or fourth time, and nodding our heads in silent agreement, our stomachs start churning and the ever-present, nagging question returns. "Will I spend this holiday alone again?" I think a lot of us even wonder if God sees our desire, or cares. How can a person want someone so bad in his or her life and still be alone?

It's tempting to play pity the card that you will be alone for the rest of your life. But before you play that card again this year, answer these questions. Why are you alone? Why haven't you found someone? Why can't you keep someone in your life? No matter how much you pray that they stay, they always leave. My friend, why does this keep happening? Are you tempted to blame yourself, lay down in your self-pity, and quit?

Something bigger
Let's look at the nature of relationships. I will try to make this as painless as possible. First, some quick ground rules. Thou shalt not cry about not having a girlfriend or boyfriend. Okay, this is not a commandment, but as we get into this discussion, you will see that this behavior can lead to keeping potential suitors away. Next, thou shalt not covet a movie star instead of what God is giving you. Thou shalt not lie or deceive just to keep someone in your life. I might be getting ahead of myself a bit and stealing from my next book, but these are just a few of the topics we need to discuss.

The easiest way to explain the nature of relationships is the element of preparing one another for each other. I guarantee that the person you thought was so cute in grade school is probably not the person you will end up with for the rest of your life. Relationships prepare us and build us for our eventual wife- or husband-to-be.

I am not your typical minister who believes you are going to date only one person and that person will be your husband or wife. If that idea were true, some of us would never have the woman or man who is in our life today. I am serious.

What's the problem?
The pros in this field say that for guys the problems in relationships are often an issue of maturity. But gals have an issue with needing to see or have a sense of security and stability. These expert opinions may be partially correct, but maturity and security aren't always deciding factors, especially when you throw love into the mix. I have seen insecurity and maturity issues on both sides. In fact, some people in their forties still have major issues about maturity in their relationships. Why? Remember that the nature of relationships prepares us for each other. Somewhere down the road, these forty-year-old adults didn't prepare themselves to handle the issues that come up in marriage. Hey, if God could give us only one person, like he gave Eve to Adam in Genesis, He would! But God knows we are picky, finicky, intolerant, selfish, impatient and so on and so on. So it makes perfectly good sense that these relationships we get in and out of can prepare us to know how to handle and treat others. God knows all your qualities, even the ones that will scare someone out of your life.

Some of us are unreasonable and impossible to spend a short time with, much less a lifetime. Please understand me when I tell you that I am not promoting dating everyone you can to prepare you quicker for the person God has for you. What I am saying is that you have to open your eyes to deal with the issues you brought to the relationships you have been in over the years. Trust me when I tell you that you are not perfect. No matter how loving and kind you think you are, you will have something that needs to be dealt with before the person God has for you becomes a permanent part of your life.

Is love really blind?
I shared previously that many of us can fall in love with just about anyone. But that doesn't mean everyone will want us the way we are today. Falling in love with someone is more than an emotional attachment. A conscious decision must be reached about whether he or she is the person for you. Truthfully, we often become so blinded by the emotional whirlwind of excitement that we tend to ignore the things that should set off the warning sirens. Sometimes we want something or someone too much and our desire becomes unhealthy.

So how do we pick a partner for life? That's the question I am always asked. Here are my suggestions:

- Choose someone who is sound emotionally. Anyone who is having a hard time emotionally will either depend too much on you or be hurtful toward you. An emotionally unstable person is usually looking for someone to vent anger or disappointment on.

- Second, choose someone with good morals. Why would you want someone who makes you guess about his or her commitment toward you?

- Third, choose someone who would complement or add to your life and vision. If they take away from your walk with God, you are not being honest with yourself about your decision. Yes, I believe people can change, but not at the expense of losing your fire and passion for the Gospel.

- Fourth, choose someone who gives back to you. Not necessarily money or material possessions, but love and respect.

If you have several candidates who fit this bill, then you're a blessed individual! If you don't, have faith that you will not be alone if it is your desire to have someone God will provide.

107

"Delight thyself in the also in the Lord; and he shall give thee the desires of thine heart" (Psalms 37:4).

Afterword

Involvement in a good church helps in building a strong, loving life with someone. Churches offer you a family outside your own comprised of godly couples and singles who have gone through similar battles. These people can share their personal experiences with you and give you wise advice. You also need to be committed to your relationship with your spouse and with God to make these principles work. Keeping godly principles in your relationship will help resolve issues in your personal life.

Now that I have offered you the church as one of the helping hands to successful relationships, let me tell you (just to be fair) what you should expect. Remember the schoolteacher you knew you could go to no matter what happened. You had plenty of teachers, but there was one who was special to you. No matter what came up or what the situation was, he or she would be there for you. You trusted him! You admired her! Even today, you still have fond memories of your favorite teacher in your heart.

This is the kind of feeling and level of trust you need to have with the pastor, pastoral staff, church members or someone from the church you attend. If you don't have that feeling, then maybe you need to try to get to know them better. Over time, a stronger level of trust and feeling may develop. Maybe you can't get the feeling there because they all know you too well or you feel you're being judged for some reason. If that is the case, you may need a group or someone on the outside to help.

A word to church leaders
I want to insert some words of wisdom to church leaders about what they can do to help hurting people. First, **DON'T JUDGE.** Nobody's perfect; we all have problems and hang ups. Second, **SHOW LOVE.** Even a child recognizes the difference unconditional love can make. Third, **FOCUS ON ALL THE FLOCK** not just the ones from whom you get a response. Sometimes people become reclusive because they feel lost in a

crowded place. Make it a point to welcome and enjoy everyone who is fellowshipping with you.

Most of us who have been saved for some time would likely reach out first to the church staff or a godly man or women. But some may be going through problems without considering asking for help. This is why those older in the faith must make themselves available. I really think we seasoned believers have become too busy. We used to have time after services to talk and fellowship with one another. Now we rush to our cars and home to lunch and the football games.

As I visited churches over the years, I noticed the same pattern in almost every church. Within twenty minutes of the final amen, the church is empty. The pastor greets you as you're leaving the church, or he is whisked away with his entourage. I think almost all churches meet, greet, and go. No, I don't expect the pastor to stay for hours just to talk to me. But it seems hard for someone to build a relationship with a church if he or she has less than twenty minutes to get to know people. Without social events, we may never get to know our church family. When is the last time you invited a visitor or a new member to lunch?

Love one another
The church has a responsibility to its people. We need to be a reachable—not returnable. This means we need to love one another like the Word of God says. In John 15:12, "This is my commandment that ye love one another, as I have loved you." No other faith is established on this principle. Christianity is known for its love. We are different. We are supposed to know how to love and forgive. It's our new nature. We need to respond in love, no matter what. They will know us by our love.

If you would like to listen to the shows that inspired this book please visit us at any of our websites.

www.revministries.com

www.midwatchwiththerev.com

www.relationshipseries.com

www.survivorsbyfaith.com

If you would like to make an appointment for faith-based Christian counseling sessions using belief therapy with "The Rev" Dr. David Yanez. Please send an email to

therev@almostoutofgrace.com

For information about setting up a Relationship Series 3 day seminar or a conference in your area please contact us.

therev@davidyanezministries.com

David Yanez Ministries
PO BOX 5172
Kingwood, TX 77325

1-888-241-0768

For additional copies of this book and other books by Dr. David Yanez please visit our website.

www.revministries.com